Audit Alchemy

When high expectations do not always match the resources at your disposal, how can small Internal Audit teams make a significant impact? This book is your essential guide to transforming the way you approach internal auditing. Professionals who lead or work in small teams in Risk, Compliance, Information Security and Quality across all sectors will also find this book especially relevant.

This book provides tools, techniques and inspiration, starting from establishing a solid foundation to leveraging technology, building strong governance, utilizing third-party support and systemising your processes for consistency, quality and efficiency.

Packed with strategies, hacks and insights from thought leaders from a variety of backgrounds and sectors, this is a relatable and empowering volume that will help you discover how to become a trusted advisor to your C-suite and Audit Committee and how to delight your stakeholders with innovative outputs and effective communication.

With fresh perspectives and real-world examples, *Audit Alchemy* aims to give you the confidence to innovate and the courage to lead.

Sandeep Das is an award-nominated, experienced Head of Internal Audit, Independent Audit Committee member and Chartered Accountant (FCA), with 20+ years of experience in Finance, Internal Audit, Risk Management, Governance and Compliance across multiple industries: Pharmaceutical Life Sciences, Healthcare, Higher Education and the Third Sector. He has held several Finance roles in industry and has been an external auditor at a Big Four accountancy practice.

Security, Audit and Leadership Series

Series Editor: Dan Swanson, Dan Swanson and Associates, Ltd., Winnipeg, Manitoba, Canada.

The scope and mandate for internal audit continues to evolve each year, as does the complexity of the business environment and speed of the changing risk landscape in which it must operate. The fundamental goal of this exciting series is to produce leading-edge books on critical subjects facing security and audit executives and practitioners. Key topics addressed include Leadership, Cybersecurity, Security Leadership, Privacy, Strategic Risk Management, Auditing IT, Audit Management and Leadership, and Operational Auditing.

Digitalization and Women's Rights Women and Sustainability: Volume 2
By Muharrem Kılıç and Sezer Bozkus Kahyaoglu

Governance, Risk and Compliance: Demystifying the Risk and Data Privacy Landscape
By Dr Michael Brass

It's Not in the Manual: Real-World Leadership for Security and Risk Professionals
By Michael Gips

Transforming Cybersecurity Audit Practices with Agility and Artificial Intelligence (AI)
By Dr. Linda Kostic

Teach, Train, Transform: The Superhero Way
By Denise Cicchella

Audit Alchemy: Small Teams, BIG Impact - A Guide to Internal Audit Excellence
By Sandeep Das

To Mayuri, Siddhartha and Purabi
For Mum and Dad

Contents

Acknowledgements

With thanks to all the kind people who generously took the time to contribute to this book and share their experiences, thoughts and insights.

Thank you to John Chesshire, Robin Clough, Tanya Coff, David Hill, Dr Stephen Hill, Si Hussain, Shahana Khan OBE, Hunada Nouss OBE, Marcus Panton, James Paterson, Gary Sommerford and Steve Stanbury.

Special shout out to Simran Wran and Harsh Singh.

And lastly, a thank you to all the people that I have had the pleasure of working with and learning from over the years.

About the Author

Sandeep Das BSc. FCA, CIA, CFE, CRMA, ACFS is an award-nominated, experienced Head of Internal Audit, Independent Audit Committee member and Chartered Accountant (FCA) with 20+ years of experience in Finance, Internal Audit, Risk Management, Governance and Compliance across multiple industries: Pharmaceutical Life Sciences, Healthcare, Higher Education and the Third Sector. He has held several Finance roles in industry and been an external auditor at a Big Four accountancy practice.

Sandeep is a Certified Internal Auditor (CIA), Certified Fraud Examiner (CFE) and Accredited Counter Fraud Specialist (ACFS) and has achieved a Certificate in Risk Management Assurance (CRMA).

Sandeep began his career in external audit in 2000 and moved to internal audit in 2007. He has strong expertize and knowledge of the pharmaceutical and life sciences industry with over 12 years of experience across three large UK, US and Japanese listed pharma companies. He has been an independent member of several Audit and Risk Committees.

He has also been an exam author for the Institute of Internal Auditors (IIA), a guest lecturer at a UK university, and spoken at European global conferences, delivered webinars and written articles and papers for various organizations.

1

THE CHALLENGE OF THE SMALL INTERNAL AUDIT FUNCTION

LEARNING OBJECTIVE

The reader will gain an appreciation of why attempting to replicate a large function will not yield the same outcomes or value. They will gain an initial understanding of the importance of thinking differently in their approach, and an introduction to some high-level concepts that they can begin thinking about.

1.1 Introduction – Small Team, BIG Impact!

The life of an internal auditor, a Chief Audit Executive (CAE) or Head of Internal Audit can be a tough one. But the real challenge in today's fast-paced, technology-driven workplace is leading a small Internal Audit function with limited resources, which can seem to be an immense and intimidating challenge. But you can succeed.

You may be a small team or even be a one-person team, but that doesn't limit your ability to make a big impact on your organization.

This goes for Internal Audit, but I am equally aware that in organizations, especially small and medium-sized enterprises, whether they be for-profit, not-for-profit, third sector, charity, public sector, etc., there are many other teams that are small but are expected to deliver a big impact. These teams include Corporate Governance, Information Security, Risk Management, Health and Safety, Quality and so on. This book is for all of you as well, and whilst the focus is on the world of Internal Audit, there are many valuable lessons and practical techniques that can be put into practice regardless of your chosen field.

DOI: 10.1201/9781003519256-1

1.2 Why You Can't Simply Replicate a Large Internal Audit Function

So, what are the challenges that face a small Internal Audit Function? It's a long list, but let's start with the ones that are top of mind based on my experience: Size of your in-house team can limit the function's ability to have a broad range of skills; your budget: to hire, use co-source and invest in technology – will be smaller in scale; ability to review and quality control will be restricted (especially if you are a one-person team); ability to perform multiple engagements at the same time; ability to divert resources to advisory work whilst still delivering the audit plan; having a IT audit function; having resource dedicated to providing data analytics to support audit engagements; finding time to meet and build relationships with your stakeholders and senior management; investing time in professional development and soft skills development; gaining a strong understanding of your business through meeting people across business units, countries, locations; and I am sure you can think of many, many more.

For the purposes of this book, a small Internal Audit function refers to teams of five or less auditors and one-person Internal Audit functions. Many will argue that functions of less than ten or less than 20 are also small, and what we discuss in this book is still absolutely applicable to those teams also. I would go as far as to say that regardless of your function's size, even if you are an Internal Audit function of 100+, many of the ideas and techniques should still be considered. A large Internal Audit function will often have a CAE, several directors, managers, senior auditors, entry-level auditors, a team coordinator, a separate IT audit sub-team, a data analytics team, audit software and data analytics software. A small Internal Audit function may just have a CAE or a CAE and two to three auditors and no audit-specific software.

As your organization grows, your aim is to grow your small function into a medium or even a large function in line with the company's growth. This is important to bear in mind when building your Internal Audit strategy and plans for the next three to seven years. For now, you will need to work with what you have. For other organizations, there may not be any planned growth in the medium or long term, and therefore, it is unlikely that the size of your function will materially change. There are many examples of this when we look at the not-for-profit sectors, for example, charities, higher education, local public sector.

Do not attempt to replicate all that a large function can achieve. Think about your Internal Audit function in your organization, and what good looks like through that lens. There is so much of the above that can be done, either on a smaller scale or with clever techniques that will achieve a similar outcome as if you had a large team, but they will need to be done differently.

Internal Audit functions in today's world are all about impact. So, start with that concept. How are you going to make a big impact in providing assurance and advisory services that your organization, and its wider stakeholders, are looking for? Your mandate empowers you to provide the Board and senior management with objective assurance, advice, insight and foresight. The Board and senior management absolutely want assurance, but what will really delight them is your ability to provide insight and foresight. Being able to deliver those will create the big impact you are looking to achieve. Much of the focus of this book will be on how to achieve these.

It is essential that you keep the Institute of Internal Auditors (IIA) Global Internal Audit Standards in mind when performing any work that you do and any techniques that you implement. Remember that External Quality Assessment (EQA) is due at least every five years, and it will come around sooner than you think. But bear in mind that the standards do refer to small Internal Audit functions and state that

> The internal audit function's ability to fully conform with the Standards may be affected by its size or the size of the organization. With limited resources, completing certain tasks may be challenging. Additionally, if the internal audit function comprises only one member, an adequate quality assurance and improvement program will require assistance from outside the internal audit function.

1.3 Why You Should Read This Book

Most books published to date on internal auditing are based on the premise of mid- to large-size Internal Audit functions, with large teams and sufficient budgets. However, many hundreds of Internal Audit functions, especially in small and medium-sized enterprises, third sector, not-for-profits, etc. must function at a very small scale. This presents numerous challenges that cannot be resolved based on the content of many of these existing books.

This book brings sound ideas and practical solutions to the thousands of auditors and CAEs who face the challenge of delivering more with less. Through my 20+ years of experience in Internal Audit, I will provide you, the reader, with tangible solutions that you can begin to implement immediately that will have a real impact on what you can deliver, how you and your Internal Audit functions are perceived and the overall value that your function will deliver to the organization you work for.

This book will act as an essential "go to" playbook for internal auditors to refer to when deciding the best course of action to take their Internal Audit functions forward and drive excellence.

My hope is that this book will be of value to new and existing CAEs of small to medium sized Internal Audit functions, as well as any auditors who work in smaller Internal Audit functions. This book would also be useful for Board and Audit and Risk Committee members wanting to learn how to get the best out of their Internal Audit functions, as well as C-Suite and senior management who liaise with Internal Audit.

It is important to note that the concepts in this book apply to all internal auditors regardless of the size of their functions and could also be useful for partners and directors who work in practice and who support their clients' Internal Audit functions in co-source or outsource models.

Many of the concepts would also be applicable for Risk Management, Compliance, Counter-Fraud and Investigations and Information Security professionals that work in smaller teams.

The book aims to be industry agnostic and be valuable to the reader regardless of industry: Public companies, privately held companies, not-for-profit, third sector, government, NGOs, etc.

1.4 How to Get the Most from this Book

This book has been structured in such a way that you can work through each chapter and think about where your Internal Audit function is at this moment, what you can implement immediately from each chapter and what you can build into plans for the next three, six or twelve months. The flow is in a logical order of taking a step back to think about your goal for your function, what you want to achieve and then how you can practically go about delivering on that vision. Starting with the fundamentals of any business function: Your remit, structure, reporting lines and budget. Then moving on to how you can use third parties to support in creating the building blocks of your function, how you can systemize your audit work to deliver your work efficiently and with consistent quality and how to deliver impactful outputs that delight your Board and senior management, create that trusted advisor relationship you have been striving for and find the courage to lead.

The final chapter brings all that we will learn together and encourages us to turn these ideas into reality and be confident in bringing them to life.

Along the way, we will also discuss areas such as how to tackle and deliver a successful Internal Audit function even when you are asked to take on additional roles, how to build in Counter-Fraud into your audit work and help create a Counter-Fraud culture across your organization, the importance of branding and marketing your function, how to get the best out of the tech available to you and how to embrace diversity and inclusion.

1.5 The Art of the Possible

By using this book and using your own skills, experience and creativity, you can achieve amazing outcomes. It will take time and effort, but you can get to a place where your small team makes a BIG impact.

Let's get started!

2
Your Team, Your Boss and Your Budget

LEARNING OBJECTIVE

The reader will gain an understanding of different approaches to structuring and managing their teams, ideas on options for reporting lines and how to ensure the terms of reference/internal audit charter can be optimally written. They will gain expertize on preparing a departmental budget and how to best present the return on investment the function can deliver to various stakeholders to ensure buy-in and support.

2.1 Governance

Let's talk about governance. Domain III of the Global Institute of Internal Auditors (IIA) standards focuses on this topic, and it is important to get this in a good place at an early stage. The standards state, "Appropriate governance arrangements are essential to enable the internal audit function to be effective." Good governance of the Internal Audit activity is not just your responsibility but also the responsibility of your organization's senior management team and the Board. All three parties need to demonstrate responsibility and accountability to ensure success.

It is not possible to simply lay down the law with regard to how you think Internal Audit governance needs to work in your organization. This needs discussion with senior management and the Board, especially if you are a new CAE coming into post, or this is the first time the organization is embarking on having an Internal Audit activity.

DOI: 10.1201/9781003519256-2

2.2 Team Structure

As a small Internal Audit shop, you often find that you are not in fact a department on your own; you are part of the Finance function or the Legal function or the Corporate Governance function. This does not sound ideal – remember that the Internal Audit activity is an *independent* function. But the reality on the ground is that you will find yourself part of a bigger team. This can actually be absolutely fine as long as there is clarity and understanding of your activity and the independence and objectivity required. It can be a gift rather than a curse. A small or one-person Internal Audit activity can feel like a very lonely place. And being part of a bigger community of professionals can be a valuable asset. No need to sit in an isolated office in the basement, away from all other functions, to physically demonstrate your independence – you now have a network, a community, of colleagues who understand you and are there to support you.

I once worked in an organization where one of the Internal Audit teams in a different region felt that they had to sit apart from other functions in the business. In an entirely different building! And this level of separation even extended to the lunch break, where the team would feel that they could not sit or converse with colleagues from other functions in the office restaurant for fear of impacting their ability to be independent. I do wonder how you can provide assurance, insight and foresight to your business when you are not empowered to actually find out about what is going on in your business through simply talking to your colleagues.

So, regardless of where you find yourself in an organization, take a step back and think about how to make it work.

2.3 Reporting Lines

Given what we have discussed above, let's think about reporting lines. In my various CAE roles, I have reported to the Chief Compliance Officer, Chief Finance Officer, General Counsel and Director of Governance. The optimal reporting line – in my personal opinion – is administratively to the Chief Executive Officer and functionally to the Audit Committee (Chair of the Audit Committee). If we refer to the Global Internal Audit Standards, it also states that:

> Organizational Independence, it is important that the chief audit executive report administratively to an individual in the organization who can support the internal audit function's pursuit of the internal audit mandate. A leading practice is for the chief audit executive to report to the chief executive officer or equivalent.

So, I have never had what I consider to be the correct, or ideal, reporting line. But I have made it work. Be flexible, be adaptable, but still be clear when it comes to independence, objectivity and the ethics of your work.

Different businesses and organizations are structured in different ways. Some may not have an Audit Committee or a Risk Committee or equivalent that provides that function line for you to report into. That does not mean that there is no value in having an Internal Audit function. Where I have pushed for changing the administrative reporting line to the CEO, there has been pushback, often from the CEOs themselves. And there are valid reasons for this. Maybe they just do not want another direct report, however important you may think they should have. They would rather have you report administratively to the CFO or General Counsel. You may well find that these individuals are more supportive of the Internal Audit mandate. A potential solution is to build in a direct line to the CEO and to make sure that the CEO wants you to always have an open door to their office if you need it. It may involve periodic meetings; for example, every two months with the CEO in addition to your line manager. This can work very well, but you need to put the work in to make this relationship fruitful for both parties involved.

It is important to ensure that Internal Audit stays close to the C-suite, and that the activity's prominence and ability to communicate directly with the C-suite are not eroded over time. The way to achieve that is through the work that you do and the value that you bring. So that rather than you pushing for it, it is the C-suite that is pushing for you to remain close to them. That only happens when your product is seen as too valuable to not be in direct sight.

You need to be pragmatic and adaptive. There needs to be education of management, clarity of reporting lines and respect for those reporting lines. But the focus is on the outcomes. Are you able to achieve what you need to achieve – and in accordance with the Global

IIA standards – with the model you have? Pushing for change when it doesn't move the needle will result in little added value and only create animosity and a lack of support for your work.

Tanya Coff (Non-executive Director and former CEO and CFO) shares her experience:

> In a previous role as CFO, the Head of Internal Audit reported to me, and this felt like a natural fit. What is most important is having a clear reporting structure and accountability to ensure the effectiveness of the internal audit function. What matters most is independent thinking, confidence to spotlight good practices and the courage to be vocal in raising concerns.

2.4 Terms of Reference

You will need a Terms of Reference or an Internal Audit Charter.

The concept of this book is to be agile, adaptive, efficient and to never reinvent the wheel. So, when you are crafting your Internal Audit Charter, use an existing template. Take a look at the templates provided by the Global IIA and Chartered Institute of Internal Auditors (CIIA), but you will also find lots of examples of actual Internal Audit Charters, as organizations often publish these on their websites. This is especially the case with the public sector.

But this is not an exercise in simply copying and pasting a template and then finding and replacing the company name with your company name. You will need to think about what the charter needs to include – the tone, length, content, etc. – that will work for your organization. It needs to be tailored and needs to be able to work for your Internal Audit activity and your organization.

Take some time to think about what to include. Then do your research to help you craft *your* charter. But don't spend too long on it. Remember, the standards require you to review them at least annually and amend and update them accordingly. As with everything, things change over time, and there is no perfect charter. It needs to work for you now, and it will change over the course of your tenure as CAE. And if it needs to change more frequently than annually, then change it. Don't wait 12 whole months. Be proactive and adaptive.

2.5 The Challenges of Leading a Team of Internal Auditors

Let's talk about your team for a moment. With a small team of in-house internal auditors, you need to be able to identify, understand and manage the challenges that this poses. A few challenges you will face include keeping the work fresh for your team, limited progression opportunities, the impact of a team member being out of the business, staff turnover and skill gaps.

Keeping Work Fresh: When you have auditors who have been in the same role for a number of years, you may find that they end up performing the same audit engagements every few years or every year. This could be because they are talented and have the experience and skillset that lend themselves to that particular audit engagement or scope. This can result in the work becoming stale and repetitive. The challenge is to keep the work fresh, and there are methods to be able to achieve this. It is important to ensure a fresh perspective each time you perform a specific audit engagement and also to maintain quality. So having a different team member perform it actually makes a lot of sense. The experienced team member can support and act as a subject matter expert but is then freed up to perform other types of audits. Given the ever-evolving nature of our assurance work, there should be new and uncharted audits for your team to get stuck into, which should hopefully ensure they are constantly challenged.

Limited Progression: A reality can be that there will be no – or extremely limited – progression for your auditors. Progression may only occur when the CAE moves on. Even then, there is no guarantee that their replacement will be from the existing audit team. The thought of years of waiting and no certainty will inevitably lead to an increased risk of team members looking for other opportunities outside of your organization. My personal view is that being a CAE in the same organization is not a job for life – you have a shelf-life of seven to ten years maximum before things start getting too comfortable. But let's be honest, no ambitious person is waiting that long to progress.

There are some considerations here. When hiring for your team, be upfront about the likelihood of progression in the Internal Audit team. Give people the opportunity to understand the situation right from the start. Think about opportunities outside of the Internal Audit function that your team may be interested in. It is very common for auditors to move into different roles – either a sideways move or a promotion – in a completely different function. Historically, this has been a move into a Finance role. That's exactly what I did a few years back when I found myself in this exact position. Looking at skillsets, and through your networks, understand what opportunities may be coming up, and if there is a potential good fit. Think project management, corporate governance, information security, quality assurance, marketing, risk, etc. Create those opportunities for your team. Some people are simply happy with their current position. They may well be brilliant at their jobs, clients like them, they enjoy what they are doing, and for whatever reason, they want to continue in the status quo and not progress. If their work is of a high quality and they come to work every day, enjoying what they do, then this is a great result.

Impact of a team member being out of the business: The reality is that in a small team, if a team member is out of the business – even for only a few weeks – this can create a significant impact on the rest of the team and the output the team can achieve. There could be many reasons for this; for example, illness, secondment, carers' leave, bereavement, etc. In a large team, one member being out for a few weeks may have minimal impact as the other team members can pick up the work. But in a small team, it can significantly affect the delivery of the audit and advisory work, and this can create added pressure on the remaining team. As a leader, you will need to have contingencies to manage this. Strategies may include utilizing co-source to bridge the gap, using guest auditors, seconding someone from another department into the function or rephasing your audit plan. You need to ensure your team does not burn out and that the quality of your audit work does not drop. This scenario is a very likely one and so make sure you have planned ahead for this eventuality.

Skills Gaps: The skills that the modern Internal Audit function now requires to perform the expected wide variety of audit scopes do not lend themselves well to a small team. There is only so much one can learn and stretch themselves to accomplish. Gaps in skillsets are another inevitability of the small team. There are some options that you can adopt from inside your organization; for example, bringing in a guest auditor who has the requisite subject matter expertize or training or developing one of your internal auditors in advance of the audit engagement. But in reality, you may have to look outside of your organization to address this skills gap. And that means utilizing your co-source or bringing in a contractor for a particular audit engagement. There are budget implications with these options, and it is your responsibility to ensure the budget is available, and management and your Audit Committee understand why it is required.

Staff turnover: This is a given in a team of any size, in any function, in any organization. The likelihood is high, and in a small team, the impact is also high. Therefore, this is a challenge you will face and need to be prepared for. When people leave, the obvious step is to recruit to backfill that position. But this will take time, and you have a gap in your team's ability to deliver the output that has been agreed with management and your Audit Committee. The strategies discussed in the above two sections can be deployed here to manage the situation while you recruit. But there are also strategies that you can adopt in advance to reduce the impact. Through your internal networks, be aware of potential good candidates who may be interested in a role in Internal Audit. Make sure your internal branding and marketing of the Internal Audit function are on point – we talk about how best to achieve this later in this book. Keep an eye on the market. Build and maintain good relationships with the key recruitment agencies in the Internal Audit space. Make sure they know what you are after if an opportunity were to arise. Finally, do your own research into candidates who may be a suitable fit, who work in Internal Audit functions at other organizations in your sector and geography. Make sure you are networking and building connections and relationships both in-person and online. These are some great ways to be proactive and effectively manage this risk.

2.6 The Positive Experiences You Must Cultivate in Your Team

Given the challenges we have discussed above, it will be up to you as a leader to create positive experiences for your team. Different people will have different approaches and ideas of how best to approach and achieve this. I will suggest a few ideas, but this is by no means exhaustive, and you must constantly work on how to cultivate your team.

Examples of the opportunities you must focus your efforts on include:

- Creating better connections within your team
- Adopting a more personal approach to work allocation
- Fostering a closer interest in team members' personal development
- Developing opportunities for exposure to senior management

Let's look at each of these in a little more detail:

Creating better connections within your team: An advantage of leading a small team is that it allows for better and deeper connections within the team. There is an opportunity and an ease for team members to get to know each other better, both professionally and personally. This can enhance collaboration and understanding of each other's strengths. As a leader, you must take time out of each day to build better connections with your team but also encourage your team to interact with each other and learn from each other. A small team can create a closer-knit and more supportive environment. Team members are more likely to support each other through challenging times, and this can only serve to enhance overall team cohesion.

Adopting a more personal approach to work allocation: You should quite quickly get to know each individual team member, their strengths, areas of development, preferred way of working, etc. In a large Internal Audit function, it is often a case of having a team coordinator look at the scheduling tool and just assigning whoever is available for a specific audit engagement, with very little, if any, thought given to who is right for that particular audit. And it can be left up to the individual auditors to fight their corner to get assigned to audits that will help their development. You can take a much more personal approach to allocating work in a smaller team. This can now be based on individual strengths and qualities, which will manifest in better quality audits and better output from you and your team. You will naturally know which team member is best suited for specific tasks.

Fostering a closer interest in team members' personal development: You have a responsibility to actively manage and support your individual team members' personal development. You should be finding a suitable amount of time to focus on one-to-one sessions with your team, and this will allow you to take a closer interest in the personal development of each team member. You will need to be an effective line manager, but sometimes also a mentor or coach. Helping and ultimately seeing your team progress and flourish in their careers will add personal satisfaction to your work.

Developing opportunities for exposure to senior management: It can be a real challenge to develop opportunities for your team to gain exposure to senior management in a large Internal Audit function. If you are a team of a hundred or more, giving each and every team member this type of opportunity simply is not feasible. However, I have seen in smaller teams, there are many ways you can find to give your team time and space to interact with and learn from senior management, the C-suite and Audit Committee members. Let me give you a couple of examples. Have one of your team members join you at an Audit Committee to field any questions that may arise about an audit they recently performed. It gives them a chance to see first-hand how an Audit Committee meeting works and a chance to meet Audit Committee members. During the annual audit planning meetings with executives or for any regular check-ins with executives, if you are unavailable to attend, send one of your team members instead. Make sure you prep them in advance of course. If you are delivering any training to the directors or the Audit Committee, have one of your team members support you with the delivery of the training. These are great options for giving your team exposure to leaders, who they may not normally have the chance to engage with; it will push them and develop them and also raise their profile in the business for when they want to make their next steps in their career.

2.7 Budgeting

Domain IV: Managing the Internal Audit Function, Standard 10.1 Financial Resource Management of the GIIA standards states:

> The chief audit executive must manage the internal audit function's financial resources. The chief audit executive must develop a budget that enables the successful implementation of the internal audit strategy and achievement of the plan. The budget includes the resources necessary for the function's operation, including training and acquisition of technology and tools. The chief audit executive must manage the day-to-day activities of the internal audit function effectively and efficiently, in alignment with the budget. The chief audit executive must seek budget approval from the board. The chief audit executive must communicate promptly the impact of insufficient financial resources to the board and senior management.

The standard goes on to provide some detail on considerations for implementation and examples of evidence of conformance.

When you create a budget for your Internal Audit activity, always keep in mind Return On Investment (ROI). And also start with the principle of a zero-based budget.

At first, you may not even own a budget or get involved in budget setting. You will need to work with your line manager and function to change this, and carve out a separate Internal Audit activity budget, your own cost centre and a direct relationship with your finance business partner and regular budget versus actuals reporting.

The organization will have a budget-setting process, and you will need to follow that.

There is a need to build your ROI proposition when pitching for more resources.

When considering your value proposition, the trick is to demonstrate the impact or potential future impact on the business as a whole. Your Internal Audit function is not just a cost centre; there are ways in which you can demonstrate how your function and your work can impact Earnings before Interest, Tax, Depreciation, Amortisation (EBITDA). Successfully and convincingly demonstrating this to your C-suite will have a profound impact on you and your work going forward. Here are some ideas on how this could be achieved.

2.8 Understanding Context

There can be a tendency to have a silo mentality when putting together your budget. Often, this can be inward-looking, that is, the focus is purely on what you and your function need, in terms of resources, people, technology and co-source/consultancy support. That is fine as a starting point. But then there is a need to consider the wider context of your business's current financial position and future financial position. Is your business growing, performing well, actively hiring and expanding into new markets and territories? Or is it in a slump, that is, not meeting investor expectations, losing money and losing market share? It is also worth understanding the wider industry and sector outlook; are you in a fast-paced high-growth industry or a more mature industry that may be stagnating?

When pitching for budget, these wider factors are essential to incorporate. Si Hussain (Finance Trainer, Author and former CEO Woodspeen Training Group Plc) offers his experiences:

> You need to understand the context of the business in which you're operating at the time in which you're asking for budget. Because even in the best businesses, great ideas can still be turned down at times when there is a strategic imperative to deliver results. So, let's say the bottom line has to hit a certain number; frankly, even if the Internal Audit function is doing a fantastic job and they are managing and controlling risk, and you are asking for money that is a definitive outflow, without there being a corresponding inflow, you are not going to get it.

So timing can be critical. And the best time to ask for budget is when times are good.

You are more likely to be successful in getting the budget you have proposed if you have got a good track record to investing it wisely and effectively. I fully appreciate that if you are just starting out, you have no track record necessarily. And this can be a challenge.

2.9 Expectation of Resource to Help you Succeed

If you are in a business where they have gone to the effort of creating a new Internal Audit function, investing time, effort and money in recruiting a Head of Internal Audit and possibly additional auditors, then you can be safe in the assumption that this investment has been made with the idea that management and the Board want the function to succeed. Now, there may have been legal and regulatory reasons why the Internal Audit function has been created; that is, it is a mandatory requirement and not a 'nice to have'; this is the case in certain industries, publicly listed companies, and certain public sector organizations.The Board or Audit Committee may have insisted on the creation of an Internal Audit function. And your C-suite, especially your CEO, may not really understand Internal Audit other than the fact that it should help them identify, manage and control risks. But it is reasonable to expect that they would consider that the function will be a positive force in managing risk, and therefore the cost-benefit should work in the business's favour. If I, as the CEO, have asked for you to come on board, then there should be an expectation that you will come to me to ask for some resources to deliver the function effectively. This is an expectation for any department in a business. The Chief Executive's natural instinct will be for your function to succeed.

2.10 Strategic Investment

Internal Audit is a strategic investment that should help a business reach its goals and objectives. Si Hussain offers the following perspective:

> As a CEO, if I have invested in something – a new department or new product or new location, etc., I would give you a minimum of three years

to deliver me something. As the CEO, I have a strategic investment view; and I know that investment always precedes return. Over the course of those three years, I'll have in my mind an expectation that you are going to come to me for some money. And my approach is I want to give you the opportunity to succeed. I am not in the business of promoting your chances of failing. I don't want my employees to fail, I want to see them succeed, because that is what makes a successful business.

2.11 How to Approach Budget Expectations

We talked earlier about how to create your budget, using a zero-based approach. The next step is how to approach and navigate budget expectations. There are several ways to go about this, and you will need to identify what will work best for your business. You could consider benchmarking, comparing the size of your business with other similar businesses in your sector and looking at the composition and budget of their Internal Audit functions. In certain industries, this data may be available, for example, the public sector, the higher education sector and the not-for-profit sector. But, in other industries, it can be difficult to obtain this data. And even if it is available, direct comparisons are often not logical to make, due to the many factors that may make your business not directly comparable. However, this can form part of your arsenal of data to support your budget request.

Another approach is to consider your risk-based annual audit plan – assuming you are opting for the more traditional approach of an annual plan. Many audit shops still opt for the one-year plan, and I have come across three-year plans, albeit with significant caveats of the need for those plans to be flexible. With a one-year or even three-year plan to hand, you can look at the number of audits you intend to perform, add on other elements, that is, advisory work, ad hoc requests, training, development, etc. And work out the number of people-days required to deliver that. This multiplied by salary, along with other general and administrative costs (think travel, accommodation, phones, hardware, software, etc.), can give you a budget figure.

And then you can consider comparing your in-house function to a fully outsourced function. So, if the Internal Audit function were fully outsourced to say one of the Big Four, based on your proposed plans and the three-year department strategy, what would the cost be?

You may have some ballpark data on the hourly and daily rates of the Big Four, and so you can work this out.

Understanding which option will best resonate with your budget approvers is important before you opt for which approach you will go with.

2.12 Building Credibility and Competence

As a new function, there is a natural credibility gap. It's not even credibility; it is a competence gap. You may think you are credible and competent. But to demonstrate this and have the people who need to believe this is hard earned.

Achieving credibility and competency starts with building relationships with people, and the reality is that it comes with time. When you are looking to have those budget conversations, you will need to put in the groundwork in advance and build up some of that credibility. Do not turn up on day one expecting people who do not know you to believe in you.

This groundwork is not just about the person who is going to approve the budget. It is actually building credibility with the people for whom that budget approver trusts to give them a view about somebody. Identify those people and start connecting and demonstrating what you can offer. So, if your budget holder is the CEO and they are sitting around the Boardroom table, they may ask their trusted advisors and fellow C-suite colleagues, "What are your thoughts on this person? What do you think about their proposal?" What you want to happen in this situation is that you have some vocal supporters who, in the best-case scenario, praise and champion you, and as a minimum, can say that they consider you to be a sensible and credible person.

Plan ahead and consider how best to make your case to deliver what you want in the most effective way. This may mean coming to the table with options. Have an ideal scenario of what you need for where you want to go. Then have some options in your back pocket; something along the lines of

> this is where we want to get to, but we can do this in steps, if you can give us this budget for now, we think we can achieve a good portion of

> our ultimate goal. And I would be happy to come back to you in a year to report progress, based on these metrics.

Have those metrics ready to present.

2.13 Demonstrating Return on Investment

Demonstrating ROI will need to be a mix of quantitative and qualitative. It is hard to do with just figures alone. It will be a combination of hard data and stats, supported by stories, case studies, projections and feedback from your clients.

What will move the needle are events that were unexpected along that three-year period, which you have managed or dealt with, or identified or prevented. You need to have the evidence to point to these events.

Benchmark your ROI against your peers, where feasible, both internally – non-revenue generating functions in your organization – and externally – other Internal Audit functions in your industry.

Si Hussain makes the following observation:

> Do not think you can use your accounting background (if you have one that is) as a competitive advantage. Do not try and blind people with numbers because you are an accountant. People will see through that straight away. You are not pitching to the CFO, your play is to the entire Board. The numbers are led by the strategy, not the other way round. Focus on the business rationale.

Actually, accountants can be very bad at presenting business information. I am saying this *as an accountant* who has fallen into this trap in the past – more than once. We can be great at presenting the numbers, but we can also be lousy storytellers.

A top tip is to have a critical friend within your organization – or even a peer outside your organization – who has experience with regards to budget approvals and lean on them for honest and harsh feedback. And use that to adjust your content and approach.

Following the above approach will place you in an excellent position to be able to credibly and continually demonstrate the ROI you and your function provide in keeping your organization safe, whilst also helping to drive it forward.

2.14 Summary

Taking the time to focus on devising your game plan and approach to governance of Internal Audit, team dynamics and ROI will help you deliver a great Internal Audit function. It will also help build that credibility and competence that your customers are looking for. But it is a moving target, and as such, you must be able and willing to pivot when necessary. Use the ideas in this chapter, but be willing to try new and different ideas because delivering a ROI – and proactively *demonstrating* that ROI – is critical for success.

3 Utilizing Third-Party Support to Succeed

LEARNING OBJECTIVE

The reader will learn how to identify the various options available of third-party support for their Internal Audit strategy, how to engage with third parties and how to obtain the best value from a limited budget. We will then go on to how to persuade the Board and Audit Committee of the need for resources to fund co-sourcing. They will also gain ideas and inspiration on how they can maximize the use of software and data analytics to improve their efficiency, product quality and impression they make with their stakeholders.

3.1 Introduction

Achieving that BIG IMPACT can't be done alone; we need help. The good news is that help is out there; we just need to know how to look for it and how to utilize it in the most efficient and effective way.

In this chapter, we are going to talk about how we will use third-party support to succeed and create what many would think can only be achieved through a large Internal Audit function, but with limited people, limited budget and lots of creativity and focus.

Before we go down the road of using third parties, which inevitably means spending money, especially when money can be tight and budgets can be limited, we need to have a vision of what we're hoping

DOI: 10.1201/9781003519256-3

to achieve, rather than engaging with third parties, before we know what we want from them.

Some of this will be the obvious: We need third parties to help us perform and deliver audits; we need third parties for subject matter expertize where we don't have these in-house; it's usually the case when we look at areas such as Technology, Information Security, Health and Safety, Quality, etc. Often, we internal auditors have a finance, accounting or business background – not a bad thing – but it may not lend itself very well to performing audits on areas that we may not feel comfortable with. A third-party partner that has this expertize and has delivered Internal Audits in these areas for other organisations would be a help. We may need expertize in terms of language skills or the ability to be on the ground in locations where we ourselves are unable to travel to – or frankly speaking – feel uncomfortable travelling to. We may need extra personnel to deliver an audit, especially if we're looking to perform several engagements at the same time, but do not have the people power to do so in-house.

3.2 Maximizing Co-Source

3.2.1 Defining a Co-Source Model

Let's talk about co-source. I am a big advocate for co-sourcing in smaller Internal Audit functions. I am actually a big advocate of co-sourcing in ALL Internal Audit functions. Let us start by defining what I mean by co-source, and this is where we have an in-house Internal Audit function that may be a standalone CAE/Head of Internal Audit, or it may be a small team where there is a CAE and one or two team members. But additionally, there is a contract in place to utilize a third-party provider to support in performing and delivering certain Internal Audit engagements alongside the in-house team. The co-source partner will use your methodology, your templates, your format, your audit approach, your branding, etc. So, for all intents and purposes, it is your own organisation's branded Internal Audit work and report that is the output. The co-source team is managed and led by the in-house team.

3.2.2 The Benefits

There are numerous other benefits that you can obtain from your co-source partner that will prove useful in driving your Internal Audit function forward and making that big impact that we are aiming for with management, with the Board, and with the wider stakeholder group. You may be surprised to hear that many of these benefits will not cost you a single penny. Here are some examples:

Management would be keen to get your thoughts and opinions on how your organization compares to others in your industry and specific sector. As a small Internal Audit function, it can be difficult to be able to obtain any data and insight on this. You should already be networking with other audit professionals in your sector, either directly or through forums, and this should help you provide useful input to your management (we will touch on this later in this chapter). However, a great way is to ask your co-source. If you have selected a great co-source partner that has significant experience in your industry and works with similar clients, they will have some insight. The key is to get them to share this, without, of course, breaching any confidentiality. You wouldn't want them to breach your confidentiality with any of their other clients. Your approach could involve informal communications with them to give you some thoughts on where your organisation benchmarks against their other clients. You may well find that they have useful anonymized data that they are willing to share.

With each specific audit engagement, you want to ensure their audit approach is thinking about the best practice they have seen elsewhere and build that into the work program and the outputs.

When planning future topics to perform audits on, you can gain knowledge about what other organizations in your sector are doing in terms of audits they are commissioning and also use this input for horizon scanning of what risks other organisations are currently focusing on.

The first two examples give you the insights, the last two examples give you the foresight to help you think ahead and share that knowledge with your senior management, the Board and also the relevant people on the ground. This should be an exercise in sharing information and foresight, not keeping it to yourself in an effort to catch people out during an audit engagement.

Your co-source will regularly publish articles and papers on Internal Audit, risk, governance, and some of these will be sector specific. Some of these will be publicly available – a top tip is to not just read those published by your co-source partner, but by other similar providers, to get a rounded view. Some papers will only be available to customers, and there are sometimes launch events, which you can attend (in person or virtually) to meet and talk to the authors of the papers and network and discuss with your peers. If you do have a small in-house team, these papers and events are an opportunity to share this knowledge with your team to support their development and broaden their skillset.

When you do come across a valuable white paper, article or report that you think may directly be useful and relevant for a particular member of the Board, senior management or just someone in a specific function, then do not be afraid to share it with them with a polite note explaining why you are doing so. It may be in relation to a new law or regulation or new technology, recent prosecution, fraud case, etc. "Just came across this useful article that I thought may be of interest." You may get a positive response, a negative response or in many instances, no response at all. You will soon learn who values this type of input, and who does not. It's an annoyance to certain people, but to others, it's a delighter that helps build your profile and tangibly demonstrates the value you bring outside of those audit engagements that people know you for.

Your co-source will hold regular events – these may be Internal Audit specific, industry specific or on broader topics, for example, the economy, tax or new legislation. These are great opportunities to learn, network and build relationships with experts at your co-source that you may not typically have had the opportunity to meet and also peers and professionals from other organizations that you can connect with and call on for advice in the future. It's a great way of ensuring you and your team are keeping up with their Continuing Professional Development (CPD). Usually, only one person in the team can attend, and that may well be the CAE. But CAEs should always look to use these events as an opportunity to let team members go instead on occasion. It is a great opportunity for development, both technical and soft skills, for example, communication or networking. Whoever attends should set up a short team meeting a day or so afterwards to disseminate what they have learnt from the event. That also covers off presentation skills as an additional soft skill that they have now learnt!

3.2.3 Building Resilience

Co-source builds resilience into your Internal Audit function. If a team member leaves or is away from work for a period of time, you can quickly bring in co-source to fill the gaps if required. If you are a one-person Internal Audit function, and you yourself decide to leave your current organization, then management and the Board have some comfort in that the function does not need to have a lengthy gap in being able to provide assurance whilst recruitment takes place. Recruitment can take several months in many countries. The co-source can be called on to continue the function. And when a new CAE joins the organization, they do not need to start from scratch, as there will be a handover and continuation from the previous CAE, via the co-source.

3.2.4 Getting the Green Light

We have identified many advantages to having a co-source support your small Internal Audit function. But if you do not have it in place already, and have never used this model, the hardest part is being able to obtain the budget to be able to make this model a success.

The first step is to lay the groundwork to make your business case for spending money. Remember, however important you may think you are, for the business and for Finance, you are a cost – along with many other functions – and you are not a revenue driver. Businesses are in the business of making money and maximizing shareholder value, which means driving the top line and being as cost efficient as possible. You are a cost of doing business. So, you will need a compelling business case and allies to support that business case.

The aim is to try and get an initial sum of money when setting the budget for the upcoming year, rather than trying to push for a change to an existing agreed budget mid-year. But before you make the request, you need to spend some time building the groundwork and making your case to the right stakeholders. Think about who in your organization are the decision makers regarding budget or who you can call on for support to get your business case agreed. This should include the Board, and you may wish to target and focus your efforts on certain Board members who you know will be open to the idea of a co-source budget. Your Audit Committee Chair and Audit Committee Members should be an obvious choice for people who will back you. For management, it would be the CEO, CFO, and certain people from the next level down from your C-suite. To make the case, you will need to explain and demonstrate the ROI. And that's the pitch – an *investment*, not a cost. If you were to receive a budget to use co-source, what would be the one, two or even three audit engagements that you would have them deliver that will create a tangible ROI that you can present to management that will make them take notice? This will be different for every organization, but some ideas of those first engagements are ones that can provide a tangible increase to top-line revenue, identify tangible cost savings, result in a significant reduction in a top risk on the corporate risk register, provide a competitive advantage that management had not identified or help management dodge a bullet of a bad decision they were about to make. In some cases, an audit engagement that literally pays for itself – that is, the returns from cost savings, tax refunds, increased revenue and increased working capital are more than the fee the co-source provider charged for performing the audit engagement. Many will say that it is not Internal Audit's role to look for cost savings or look for opportunities to increase revenue, and that we should focus on those critical risks. Maybe that's right. But it is a means to an end. Demonstrating value that your stakeholders understand and care about will help you in the long term to secure the budget to focus on those critical risks. Our role is to enhance and protect, and for too long, we have focused on protecting, often without a thought to cost.

After that successful first co-source engagement, this should help support ensuring that budgets can be approved for their use going forward. Deciding how much money you require can be tricky. You should take a zero-based budgeting approach, thinking about your plan ahead for the next year, but also your long-range Internal Audit plans, that is, the next three to five years. Will you require your co-source provider to deliver all the audit engagements on your plan, some of the audit engagements, or simply work alongside your existing team for each engagement? It is important to think this through and then work out how much you believe you will need. When working with your finance team/finance business partner, never forget the obvious rule of budget-setting. Work out how much you think you will need in the coming financial year and then add on a certain percentage (10–20%). Then wait for finance to push back and ask you to make savings/reduce your budget. Argue fiercely that you cannot reduce any further, but eventually compromise and reduce your budget by 5, 10 or 15% getting you to the number you need to deliver your audit plan. Once that budget is in place, and the co-source becomes established, it then becomes difficult for management to completely remove that budget line. Once it's in, it's in.

3.2.5 Selecting a Co-Source Partner

A budget has been agreed. The next step is to select a co-source partner. If you have gone down the route of performing a proof-of-concept where you have used a co-source partner to deliver one Internal Audit engagement, and that has been a success, then they may well be the partner for you.

Depending on the level of intended spend and your organization's Procurement Policy (which I am sure you have read and are familiar with), you will most likely need to go through a full tender process, with the support of your Procurement function.

The tender process will follow a typical process that many will be familiar with, and it is the role of your Procurement function to support you and lead the entire process. As an internal auditor, it can be a great opportunity to get a firsthand understanding of your organization's procurement process and controls; no doubt an area you will be auditing in the near future!

You will need to get an idea of the providers that are available in your region/country and an idea of those that you would like to work with or have heard from your peers or from your own past experience are great partners. The process often starts with an expression of interest (EOI), whereby you test the market by reaching out to eight to ten co-source providers to see if they are interested in tendering to win your business. Not all will, and there could be many reasons for that;

for example, their own capacity, conflicts of interest, lack of industry experience in your sector, etc. There are the usual suspects, the Big Four accountancy practices, the top 20 audit firms and a whole host of medium and small providers. Once you have whittled down your potential partners based on their interest in pitching, the next activity to work with your Procurement team on is an Invitation to Tender that clearly states all the requirements you will require from the successful vendor. Ensure that this is a broad church of what you will/may require over the next few years, thinking about where you want to take your Internal Audit activity and thinking about the strategy and goals of your organization over the next five to seven years. Your organization may well have a three-year (or longer term) strategy that you should ensure you are familiar with to ensure this is built into your requirements. Examples of this include if your organization is planning to expand into certain continents, countries, or territories in the next few years, you will want your co-source provider to have a presence in those countries. If your organization is planning to move to be more tech-based or move into a new sector or new product lines, supply chain model, etc., then again you want your future co-source partner to have that expertize and experience in the bag. Always think ahead. And use the tender process to test whether your potential partners really do have the experience and can walk the walk!

The next step will involve reviewing some hopefully very impressive proposal documents from each of the vendors interested in winning your business and then having them come in and pitch directly to you to help you make the best decision.

It is important to have a clear scoring mechanism based on several criteria when performing your assessment. It is not just about cost. You should consider scoring for factors such as industry experience, similar clients, geographical footprint, expertize in data analytics, experience of the engagement leader and the immediate team. Many firms offer very similar levels of expertize and pricing, and often it is the direct relationship between you and the engagement partner and key account manager that is essential. This should be tested during a face-to-face pitch to ensure there is rapport and that the partner is credible. As your company may not be used to being audited using a co-source model, it may be important to get management/C-suite buy-in with your decision-making and ultimate choice of co-source.

A great way to do this is by having at least one C-suite member and Audit Committee member join the final pitches, and if they are happy to do so, score the pitches. These scores can then be compiled and reviewed to get a broader view to help make that final decision. By having C-suite and Audit Committee involvement, you are ensuring they have been involved in the process and are on board from the very start with your choice of co-source partner.

Once you have scored all the pitches and discussed internally, and made a final decision, leave it to your Procurement team to handle the negotiations, and then your Legal function to get the contract in place. The next step is onboarding.

But before we get there, another option is to select more than one co-source partner. There is no rule that says you must have just one co-source partner. You always have the option to select two or more. There are pros and cons to this. The pros being wider expertize and different pricing tiers, so that you can select the right partner at the right cost for individual audit engagements based on the requirements. If one firm has much more expertize in, say, cyber, you would select that partner for that engagement. If you were looking to perform a fairly standard audit, for example, payroll or accounts receivables, and both firms could comfortably do a good job based on the scope, you could select the lower cost partner for that engagement. The cons are that you may find that because each firm is getting a lower amount of work from you, their pricing will be less competitive compared to if they were your exclusive provider. There is extra time required to make that selection at the start of each audit engagement, and time is a precious resource for a small function. A key value proposition from co-source is the understanding they build of your business, your audit clients, your Audit Committee and those relationships they have with people across your business – as an extension to your in-house team. This is harder to achieve when working with more than one co-source partner.

3.2.6 Managing a Co-Source Relationship

When managing a co-source partner, it is important to remember that it is a partnership, and you want them to be part of your team and understand your business to be able to provide the best value. This will take time but taking the time to properly onboard is essential.

Your provider should have already detailed how they plan to onboard as part of their pitch. They should be meeting you and your team, key C-suite and Audit Committee members and even going through the onboarding that a new employee of your organization would – perhaps even the mandatory training – to get a real feel for the business. They should be visiting the head office and other key sites. This will help them to understand your organization's strategy and goals.

The key processes that you must have in place from the start include:

- Agreement on the process for agreeing on audit engagement scopes
- Robust review of billing and invoices
- Regular meetings with the engagement partner
- Planning ahead for contract renewals, re-negotiating rates
- Whether to create a contract for each audit engagement or work from a Master Services Agreement (MSA), with a Statement of Work drawn up for each engagement based on the terms set out in the MSA
- Level of involvement you expect to have in each engagement

The whole process is a learning journey, and you may most likely find that over time you will change the initial model you had adopted, your co-source partner(s), level of use, etc. This is fine; there is no one right way. It must be the way that works best for your Internal Audit activity and provides the best value for your organization.

3.3 Developing Data Analytics Capability

3.3.1 Buying in Data Analytics

We, as Internal Audit professionals, have talked about the importance of data analytics for the past 20-plus years! But many Internal Audit functions, especially small ones, have struggled to implement any use of data analytics or have managed some to a very limited scale. As a small team, there are many pitfalls to attempting this, and I will talk you through some of these and hopefully provide options for a path that will work.

But somehow, someway, we must do it. It is no longer a nice-to-have; it is a necessity.

Robin Clough, Managing Director at DataConsulting, offers the following perspective: "It can be all about mindset to be honest, because there really is no reason why people can't be using data analytics regardless of the size of their team."

Firstly, look at your current Internal Audit team members.

Do any of them have the skillset, ability, interest and will to perform data analytics? But be wary of the key-person dependency this will create. If this person moves to a new role either inside your organization or to another organization, then you are literally back to square one.

Can you do it yourself? Perhaps you can, but as a CAE, is this really the best use of your time? I would suggest not.

Can you get support from another function in your organization that is already well-established in performing data analytics?

Robin Clough's views on this are:

> Where people can go wrong is when they take the approach of training every member of their team in data analytics, without necessarily identifying individuals who have the aptitude and the appetite to do it. And it's almost well, we did all the training, now we all need to do some data analytics. But then no one's actually providing any direction or strategy as to how we're then going to deploy and use those skills that we've just spent lots of money acquiring. There needs to be a plan in place after the training. Don't train everyone, train the right ones. Identify the people that are enthusiastic about it and empower them to drive it forward.

When it comes to data analytics software, there are an ever-increasing number of providers that focus on the analytics side or the visualization side. If starting from scratch, start with Microsoft Excel and Power BI. You should already have these in your organization, and there will be no added cost to you for using these. And people in your organization will already be familiar with them, so seeing and using something that is well established helps. Excel has come a long way in the past few years, and it is now a powerful tool that really can deliver a good array of analytical techniques that will support a large chunk of the first-step analytics that internal auditors are looking to implement. Consider other specialist software if other functions in your organization are using them. Look at your Tech teams, Business Intelligence teams, Business Development teams, etc. Reach out and find out how they are performing and presenting their analytics work.

If you are really lucky, you may find that:

a. You have a team member who can do the work and
b. Your organization has already purchased the software, and all you need is an additional licence (which will hopefully be a manageable cost).

An option is to get one of these teams to support your analytics work; could they work with you to build some analytics, or you, in effect, outsource the data side of the analytics, and your team focuses on auditing the output? This can be difficult to achieve, as this would be an added role for someone to take on, and their manager and team may not be happy to allocate that time. But there are options to make it work:

- Could you cover the cost of that individual's time from your budget?
- Could it be seen as a learning and development opportunity for that team?

A model that I have found works well and delivers results for our small Internal Audit functions is to use a third party. There are a few options for third-party support when it comes to data analytics.

You could choose to go with your current co-source provider. The positives are that you already have a contract in place with them, you know they are capable of the work, they know your business, and you have a good relationship with them already. The cons are that this is typically more expensive than the other two options I have in mind. They may not be as agile as you need them to be, that is, quick ad hoc analytics, and it will be more of a case of a specific analytics audit engagement or building in some analytics into an already agreed-upon audit engagement.

You could look to bring in a contractor, a stand-alone individual who specializes in performing analytics. This may allow more agility and a more acceptable price point, but it is a key dependency risk.

Finally, you can use a specialist data analytics and consulting firm to support your work. Through trial and error of trying different models, this is my preferred choice – not saying that it should be yours. The benefits of this approach are the price point, the flexibility and agility to call on them whenever needed; they will have a pool of resources so that you are not reliant on one individual, they will have other similar clients and will be able to share ideas, insights and best practices with you. There may be different pricing models, for example, contracting engagement by engagement or contracting for a certain number of days by month or quarter, so that you have a data analytics team of experts on demand as and when required. They will support with the analytics, with the visualizations, with liaising with the relevant function in your organization to obtain the raw data sets, etc.

And your focus can then be on innovation and ideas: What it is you want to achieve, how to ensure it lands well within your organization or storytelling – with the help of the visuals.

3.3.2 How to Start Getting the Best Out of Data Analytics

Now that you have your data analytics capability model in place, what data analytics are you actually going to do? If it is your first time attempting this, the aim is to prove that it can work and that it can make a real tangible impact. It is all about impact. This is how you can get management on board.

We are going to:

- Get some money back for the organization
- Make future cost savings
- Root out fraudsters
- Identify revenue opportunities.

All these tangible results will impress management and give them the trust in you to keep building on your data analytics journey.

Here is what we are going to do:

Start with the low-hanging fruit. And that is the following areas:

1. Travel and expenses
2. Procurement to payment
3. Payroll
4. Revenue

First, we need to gain an understanding of the processes, software systems and data quality in each of these areas. You may have some of this information already, through previous audit engagements; most organizations that have had Internal Audit functions established for a few years will have audited these four areas at some point in the recent past. So, hopefully, you know what software systems are being used and what quality of data can be obtained. But if you do not have this information to hand, you will need to find out. Start by identifying and speaking to the relevant functions and process owners.

Most medium to large organizations will use software for managing expense claims. These may well vary in terms of quality and functionality. You may already have an idea of this, because as an internal auditor, you will most likely have done a fair bit of travel as part of your role, and in doing so, claimed expenses. So, you should know the software and how to make a claim.

Now, when I first started as an internal auditor, we would select haphazard or random samples of expense claims to test. Often, a sample of 25. And root through boxes and filing cabinets to obtain the paper copies of the claims, along with all – or hopefully some – of the receipts attached. We would then perform a laborious manual exercise of checking receipts back to the claims, and against the Expenses policy to identify any anomalies, breaches or potential fraud. And reach a conclusion based on this sample testing. If that business had an average of 2,500 expense claims submitted each year, we have just spent several hours, if not days, testing a pitiful 1% of the population.

With 100% of the data, you will be testing every single expense claim – a 100% sample. Here are a few ideas of what we can now achieve through data analytics testing:

- Potential duplicate claims
- Unapproved claims
- Incorrect approver
- Round sum claims
- Inappropriate vendor
- Excessive mileage

In fact, anything outside of what the expenses policy says, for example, limits for meals, hotels, flights, trains, etc.

But we can also use the data to not just look for fraud or out-of-policy claims, but we can also use the data to create the insight and foresight that we will be able to use to impress management and prove our worth. Let's look at expenses broken down by vendors. Are there vendors that are not on the preferred supplier list? Are there vendors that we are constantly using where we can negotiate better rates? Assessing spend on hotels, meals and travel, can we perform a scenario analysis to flex the current spend limits in the policy that could offer cost savings?

These extra steps are where we can provide the value that delights our clients.

Final thoughts from Robin Clough that I think are essential to heed are:

> As a small internal audit function, **you have to be the pioneer**, because you simply cannot rely on the old ways of working. You are not going to have a big team to do all of that. So you almost have to start from the mindset of we're going to have to do it differently. We're going to have to be data-driven to deliver the insights. Otherwise, we're not going to be able to get the levels of coverage across the organization required to deliver what our customers want. Do things that will make the business stop and think – "That's amazing! We need to be doing that!" – Once you have wowed them, you then should work on the opportunity to hand over the goods, if you like, in terms of, you've created something that's generating useful insights about controls and processes and the business then take that data analytics over, as a second-line activity.

You start out with small steps on your data analytics journey, and as that journey progresses, you help improve processes and controls, stop fraud, save your organization money, find new revenue opportunities and deliver advanced technological solutions that make first- and second-line functions more efficient.

Now that sounds like making a big impact to me.

4

Systems to Simplify and Become More Efficient

LEARNING OBJECTIVE

The reader will gain insight and inspiration in ways of making their function more efficient, consistent in quality of output and resilient in the face of changing teams, management and budgets. They will gain practical examples of best-in-class audit manual content, templates to enhance their work and ideas for how to automate and utilize AI. They will gain an understanding of what options would work best to enhance resourcing through options such as guest auditors and micro-placements.

4.1 Introduction

The key to an effective and successful Internal Audit function is consistency. Consistency in your approach, consistency in the work performed and consistency in the quality of the output – your end product. Get this right, and you will be on your way to success.

The way to achieve this when you are a small Internal Audit function is to systemize everything you do. But do not compromise on innovation, creativity and risk-taking. It is possible to achieve both. And here is how you do it.

DOI: 10.1201/9781003519256-4

4.2 Audit Manual and Templates

We have already covered the Internal Audit Charter, which sets out your stall, your remit, your role and your accountability. So, the next step is to systemize by creating your Internal Audit manual. No more than 20 pages, please. And less if possible. Even if you are a one-person function, it still helps immensely to have a manual – it ensures consistency, it speeds up the work you do and, when your team grows, it is ready for new team members or even guest auditors to use. It will definitely help when it comes to the all-important EQA and when you need to explain to your stakeholders your methodology.

What are we going to include in our Internal Audit Manual? Firstly, explain why you have a manual in the first place. These will be for the reasons we have discussed above, but you may also have your own reasons to add. My top tip is to include a section on "how to use this manual" to make it simple and clear to the reader (and that includes yourself) and how one should make best use of the manual to ensure their work adheres to the GIIA standards, your expectations and ensures efficiency – don't reinvent the wheel, when many of the answers that you need are already here for you to use.

I would advise including the following sections in your manual: Explain Internal Audit's remit and authority, how it achieves its independence and objectivity, how the function will ensure adherence to the current applicable professional standards, the expected/required proficiency of the Internal Audit team members, how the function will use external specialists (if applicable), how it intends to interact with other assurance functions in the organization (think about the second line; finance, health & safety, quality, clinical, R&D, manufacturing, etc.), and how it intends to interact with the external financial auditors. Then, move on to actually conducting audit engagements: What is your methodology, and how should risk assessment and audit plans be created? Given the move away from annual Internal Audit plans, what are the expectations, for example, three-month audit plans, six-month rolling plans? Do not overcomplicate this and ensure that it is flexible. You may find that there is some work to do here to explain and convince your Audit Committee of this move away from the traditional annual audit plan. Many committee and Board members still expect this, but it is our role to engage with them and explain the benefits of moving away from this traditional and clunky approach.

Next is to explain the different engagement types, for example, the standard Internal Audit engagement, advisory work, continuous auditing, investigations, etc. This section does depend on your agreed remit, but there needs to be an advisory element; it can't just be performing Internal Audits.

Then work your way through explaining the approach for a typical audit engagement: Engagement planning, scoping, kick-off, fieldwork, documenting work papers, status meetings, closing meetings, drafting the audit report (or whichever format you choose to use to *communicate* the engagement results), management action plans and report issuance.

Explain how you intend to follow-up and ensure the agreed management action plans are implemented in a timely manner. And what will you do if they are not implemented, or delayed or worse still, ignored? What approach will you take to hold management's feet to the fire? From the more practical perspective, how are you going to record, track, update and report on management actions? Making this process as simple, consistent and automated as possible will save you an immense amount of time and effort and allow you to focus on more important value-add tasks, rather than administrative activities.

A section that is often the most contentious and difficult to navigate is audit engagement ratings and overall opinions. This needs to be clearly stated in your manual, with the rationale explained, as this is where your stakeholders will create the most amount of trouble for you, and you will need to be able to stand your ground and explain your reasoning. Having it documented takes away some of their ammunition. There is no one right answer, and even if you do have an agreed approach, it doesn't mean that you should stick to it forever – things change, and so should your approach to opinions and ratings.

A real-life example I often share is when I have given an overall audit opinion, without realizing the perception and expectation people may have outside of, say, local management. The expectation was that a red-rated audit report required management responsible to be fired. This, of course, was not my expectation! My intention was to draw attention to the need to focus on the urgency of the risks and address these as soon as possible through the current management and any additional support they may need to improve the internal control environment. In my mind, no one should be losing their job over an Internal Audit I have performed.

Even in a small audit function, it is critical to have a Quality Assurance and Improvement Plan. Simply writing this down will help you think about how you can ensure quality in such a small team and get you thinking about how you can get into the mindset of continuous improvement for both your function and, indeed, yourself. Both are, of course, closely linked if you happen to be a one-person Internal Audit function!

Finally, you need templates for all of the above. This is the key driver that will deliver incredible efficiency, consistency, quality and speed of output.

4.3 Audit Process Templates

What templates should you consider? I would suggest to start with the following.

4.3.1 Audit Notification E-mail Template

You have an audit plan and need to inform people each time you plan to deliver or begin performing an audit engagement. One of the best ways to do this is via an e-mail to all the relevant stakeholders, senior management and clients. Save yourself time and effort by having a template for what this notification looks like already prepared. This way, when it comes to issuing this, all you will need to do is update the title of the engagement, high-level scope, agreed timelines and the distribution list of who the e-mail needs to go to. How you communicate to your clients and wider stakeholders that you are performing an audit is important. Many people will be nervous, afraid and concerned about being audited – and you must be cognizant of people's reactions to this email. It can set the tone for the entire audit engagement process, and you want to start out on the right tone. Always consider your company culture, but I would suggest moving away from the very formal wording that is often used, and in fact, I have used in the past. You need to explain why you are performing the audit, and what benefit it can bring to the clients. It is a chance to bust some myths about audits and also your audit team. Be personable, even consider going as far as including pictures of you and the audit team with a short bio, so that clients know who they will be meeting, and start to feel like you are real, regular people!

4.3.2 Scoping Memo Template or Terms of Reference

Again, there is an opportunity here to use a standard template for this. The scoping memo template should include:

- A brief background description of the audit engagement.
- The purpose of the engagement.
- Include a list of all the areas you intend to provide assurance over and their associated key risks. I often like to document my risks in the "if," "then" and "resulting in" format.
- Once you've identified the risks, list the scope areas to be included in the audit engagement.
- Provide some detail about the audit approach.
- The audit team, who will be leading the audit, for example, will this be yourself, will this be someone in your team, will it be performed by your co-source partner or will it be a mixture of all of the above. Here again is an opportunity to include headshots and short bios of the team.
- List out all the milestones, including: (i) Receiving agreement on the scoping document, (ii) when you will begin the field-work, (iii) when you will complete the field work, (iv) when you will hold the closing meeting and (v) when clients can expect a draft audit report or memo to be circulated for their review.

Use the same format each time. People will then become accustomed to what they expect to see from your audit scoping work. It will allow them to digest the information more efficiently and respond in a timely manner with any queries or questions that they may have prior to gaining agreement. Look to align with your company branding, fonts and colour schemes. You should be able to obtain this from your Internal Communications team, or you may find helpfully that these templates are available on your company intranet. This gives this, and all, your documents a familiar feel and it helps clients to understand that you are an integral part of their company and are working with them, not against them.

4.3.3 Risk and Control Matrix

This also doubles as your audit programme. There are numerous formats that can be used. Still, a popular option is the good old spreadsheet. Smaller Internal Audit functions are especially unlikely to have any audit software, and so you must make do with what software you do have at your disposal. A spreadsheet will suffice. Some may even consider a Word document, as long as you have a tool to document the matrix. Here is where you will list out the scope areas, the associated risks, and the corresponding processes. For each process, you will want to document the controls and control owners for each scope area. Then, alongside each of those scope areas and risks, you will have your audit programme and tests. These are the tests against those controls to be able to decide if they are designed effectively, and if so, are they operating effectively.

At this point, it is also a great opportunity to think about fraud risks. Include a column that gives you and your team space to consider and document any specific fraud risks with that particular scope area and process. There may not be any fraud risks, but if there are, think about what controls you would expect to see in that process to prevent and detect those specific fraud schemes. A brilliant way to get you and your audit team thinking about the types of fraud that could occur in the specific audit engagement and specific process is to use the ACFE Fraud tree (www.acfe.com). This is a great quick reference document that lists numerous fraud schemes under the broad headings of corruption, asset misappropriation and financial statement fraud. The ACFE Fraud Tree is also a useful reference document throughout the course of an audit engagement.

It's also an opportunity to do exactly the same thing with culture. Add a column that looks at the cultural risk for each of the scope areas. Now, there may well be none that you can identify at the planning stage, but there may well be some; this gives you an opportunity to think about this at an early stage as to how you could build that into your audit programme and your test plan. There will be a number of quick reference guides that you can obtain or indeed create yourself to assist in identifying cultural risk. This type of risk can often feel less tangible to us auditors; so, identifying these risks comes with practice and experience.

4.3.4 Document Request List

As part of the planning, it is critical to use a standard template to list all the documents, information and access requests, etc. that you will require to execute this audit engagement. This should include the dates of when you would expect each item to be provided and the dates of when you actually received them. You should also include who the responsible person is for providing information. This will be a useful document to use as part of the planning, but also throughout the course of the audit. Keeping a constant track of this helps with an audit trail to identify any delays, and also to chase clients, for example, at fieldwork daily stand-up meetings or status update meetings. Again, this could be a spreadsheet to keep it really simple or there may be tools such as Microsoft Lists or bespoke software that help with this. Your co-source may well already have a portal that they use for secure file transfer; as the name suggests, this allows secure transfer of files, with restricted access, and minimizes the data security risk. You do not want lots of documents flying back and forth to various people via email. The portal will also have an audit trail – no more arguing with the client as to what they did or did not provide and when! If you are looking at doing this yourself in-house and you do not have a specific tool for secure transfer, then something like a SharePoint site will absolutely get the job done.

4.3.5 Audit Test Plan/Working Papers

If you are lucky enough to have a good Internal Audit or Governance, Risk and Compliance (GRC) software tool in place, then this is what you should be using to create your detailed audit test plan and your associated workpapers. If you do not, and to be honest, most smaller audit functions and or new audit functions will not have audit software, then it may well be good old Microsoft Excel. Or you may use a mix of Excel and Word. Excel has been my tool of choice when I have worked in functions that did not have audit software. It lends itself well to creating risk and control matrices, test plans and working papers. Word can be useful when you are documenting meeting minutes or interview minutes. A flowchart mapping tool, such as Visio, can also be a helpful addition. The key principle remains the same, which is to have a standard template to use for all your audit engagements. The uniform structure and methodology will ensure consistency of output, efficiency and quality.

4.3.6 Kick-off, Status and Closing Meetings

We talked earlier about using the same format each time to help clients become accustomed to what they expect when being audited. This goes for the front-facing output that your clients will see, that is, kick-off (opening), status and closing (exit) meeting decks. Continue to align with your company branding, fonts and colour schemes. You may have your own "internal audit" branding and logo to add to these documents. If you have templates for these, this will save you and your team hours of work during the audit fieldwork. It ensures consistency so that your auditors know what to include in these presentation decks. It ensures that your clients become familiar with these critical elements of your audit. Keep these presentation decks short and sharp. You must be able to use these as tools to deliver your message clearly and quickly. There are some schools of thought that we should move away from creating presentation decks, especially for kick-off and status meetings, due to the time and effort required to create these. This approach may well work for some audit shops. However, from my perspective, I still prefer to use them. The reasons being:

- It can be a time saver, in that the audit findings that you articulate in status meetings and closing meetings can be directly lifted and inserted into the final audit reports, thus saving time during the reporting part of the audit process
- It aids the conversation during the meetings as it gives the clients and audit teams something to refer to on screen when discussing
- It acts as a tangible product that clients can take away and refer to if they need to look at it at any point during the audit process

- It acts as evidence that these meetings and discussions took place
- Often, certain clients and stakeholders are not able to attend all the kick-off and status meetings, and this is something that can be shared with them after the meeting to read through and then giving them the option to reach out to the audit team if they have any questions. This is often a useful approach with senior folks who often do not prioritize these meetings.

4.3.7 *Audit Report or Audit Memo (or whichever format you choose to use to communicate the engagement results)*

The Global IIA Standard 11.3 Communicating Results states:

> The chief audit executive must communicate the results of internal audit services to the board and senior management periodically and for each engagement as appropriate. The chief audit executive must understand the expectations of the board and senior management regarding the nature and timing of communications. The results of internal audit services can include:
>
> - Engagement conclusions.
> - Themes such as effective practices or root causes.
> - Conclusions at the level of the business unit or organization.

Let's be honest, it is very likely to be an Internal Audit report or Internal Audit memorandum, created in either Word or PowerPoint. There will of course be other ways that you communicate your results e.g. the closing meeting presentation deck, verbal communication with management, your Audit Committee papers. But I am guessing your C-suite and Audit Committee will want you to produce a standalone report to communicate the results of each audit engagement.

There is a lot of thought leadership and ideas on this very thorny topic, but for the purposes of this section which focuses on templates, my advice is to create a template for your audit report and your audit memorandum. However, there is a need to be creative with each and every audit engagement, and your report should be flexed and adapted to suit how best to communicate the results of that particular engagement. You must also consider what will land well with your primary customers, your C-suite and your Audit Committee.

A template will help ensure consistency of output, efficiency and quality, but do not let that stifle your creativity. Make sure you are constantly looking for new ways to present and communicate your results. Be visual, be concise and be vocal.

4.3.8 Circulate Draft Report for Review by Client

Similar to the audit notification email, having a template for when you are ready to circulate the draft audit report and request management action plans can act as a great time saver. Very little brain power required. Use the template, populate it to be specific to this particular audit engagement and send. Also consider creating a template for the (inevitable) chaser email for when clients have not responded in the timeframe you had set for them.

4.3.9 Report Issuance Email

Create a well-crafted template for this email. It is the one that your primary customer is going to receive and read. Keep it short, tell the reader that you are issuing the final audit report and tell them what the outcome is; that is, what the overall rating is. Include two sentences explaining the good and the bad, that is, what has led to this overall rating. State that the management has agreed to deliver the actions, and that you will be following up and reporting on these actions. Encourage recipients to read the Executive Summary and full report. That's it, no more than two paragraphs; be brief, be bright and be gone!

With all of this, remember that your Internal Audit manual should be a living, breathing document that is regularly reviewed and updated. So, don't worry too much if version number one is not perfect; it is not meant to be. Just get it down on paper and start working with it. Then, over time update, iterate and improve. Remember, our profession is changing at a significant pace, and so must the way we work.

4.4 Automation, Standardization and Artificial Intelligence

You do not want to be reinventing the wheel each time you perform an audit engagement. A high-quality Internal Audit software package can often be a good solution to help prevent this. But you may not have one as yet. Fear not, there are still some great ways to automate and standardize your audit engagements, and indeed your advisory engagements.

If you have created your Internal Audit manual, and all the templates that should go along with it, then you are halfway there.

Technology is moving at such a rapid pace that some ideas that I share here may have already been surpassed or even become everyday common practice. But as of the here and now, let's talk about Large Language Models (LLMs) and conversational chat interface apps, that is, AI Chatbots or AI Agents.

I would argue that one of the biggest failures internal auditors are guilty of over the past 20 years is not embracing and utilizing to the maximum extent current technology. This does not apply across the board, but I hear so many internal auditors and CAEs refer to data analytics as new. Much of it has been around for 20+ years. Often, it is the smaller audit shops that fall behind in not embracing new tech. There are a number of reasons for this: lack of in-house skillset, lack of budget to invest and lack of time to invest in training and development because there is so much to deliver in just keeping up with the expectations of the day job, not knowing what is out there, as they have not seen what other Internal Audit functions are doing.

It is now a case of evolve or die. This is not an exaggeration.

Here are some examples of what you could consider when it comes to automating using AI.

4.4.1 Internal Audit Engagement Planning

Use an application, such as Co-pilot or ChatGPT, which are AI applications that use LLMs and Natural Language Processing (NLP) to help streamline workflows, automate tasks and enhance productivity. During the planning phase of an Internal Audit engagement, here are some tasks that your AI assistant can help you with.

- Background research, both internally in your organization and externally, outside of your organization. It can search and provide a summary of any relevant policies, procedures, reports, articles, incidents, etc. from inside your organization. It can also provide a summary of previous Internal Audit engagements performed.
- You can ask it to perform research and summarize any relevant laws, regulations, news articles, white papers, etc. from across the internet to help input into your audit scope and risk consideration.
- It can help you draft planning memos/audit engagement terms of reference.
- Ask it to provide ideas for suitable Internal Audit tests based on the scope and risks you plan to include.
- Review any documents you have received from the client as part of the planning process and provide a summary of key elements to include in your audit work
- Perform an initial run of data analysis to identify trends and anomalies that may guide your testing.
- For planning meetings – use it to create meeting minutes, record actions and provide meeting summaries – which can be very useful to share with your clients so that there is visibility and agreement on what has been discussed and agreed.

4.4.2 Internal Audit Engagement Fieldwork

- Create first drafts of your audit test plans and work papers.
- Based on the datasets you have received from your clients, use AI to make an initial sample selection based on your criteria and what internal controls you are testing for.
- LLMs and NLP lend themselves very nicely to helping you review a large volume of wordy documents. For example, contracts, policies, free text in datasets you have. Be clear on what you want it to look for and the output you require.

4.4.3 Internal Audit Engagement Reporting

- To assist you with communicating the results of your audit engagement, why not see if you can use AI to create a first draft of your audit report straight from lifting the findings identified and documented in your audit workpapers?
- Ask AI to draft the audit report Executive Summary.
- Use AI avatar software to create a video recording of the audit's Executive Summary. There is software that can create engaging short videos with avatars to present your audit report and findings. The video only needs to be two to three minutes in length and will really grab the attention of your clients, C-suite, and Audit Committee. They will be much more likely to watch the video, and you will gain great engagement. An added bonus for those of you working in global organizations is that the software can have the avatar speak in multiple languages. Need to create an executive summary in English, Hindi, Mandarin and Japanese – no problem!

4.4.4 Other Internal Audit Activities

- Create a first draft of your Audit Committee paper based on the recent audit and advisory work performed. Get some help in writing it more formally, less formally, more concisely, etc.
- Create some comms and articles for marketing and raising awareness of your Internal Audit function. These can be for your company's intranet site, social media network or for upcoming internal events.
- Create an Internal Audit Artificial Intelligence Agent. An "IAAIA" if you will! This can be a customer-facing AI Agent that all your clients and company employees can access to answer questions regarding your IA function, its remit, its processes, etc.
- Create an AI agent to perform the follow-up procedures for chasing open management actions, collate evidence for follow-up review and create reporting on the status of management actions.

Once you have started to experiment with these ideas, and found the ones that are working well, and are providing you with real value in terms of efficiency and insight, then you build these into your standard processes, so that they become business-as-usual in all Internal Audit engagements you perform.

There are, of course, many caveats to consider when using AI to support any of your work. Never fully rely on AI output and always perform your own review and check when it comes to truth and accuracy.

4.5 Guest Auditors, Secondments and Micro-placements

How can you increase your headcount, skillsets and output at no additional cost? Well, for a period of time at least. This could be a real benefit if you are operating as a small function. I am going to share three practical ways you can achieve this! Sounds too good to be true? Well, it's not.

4.5.1 Guest Auditors

I have been using guest auditors for years, and when done well, it brings a whole host of benefits – for your Internal Audit function, your guest auditor and your business. What is a "guest" auditor? Simply put, it is someone from another department within your organization who joins your Internal Audit team for a short, defined period of time to assist with a specific audit engagement.

There are a few pieces of this puzzle that you need to work on to get this to work effectively. Let's start with what audit engagements you have coming up in the next six to 12 months. Think about what skills you will require from your auditors. Are there any skills that you currently do not have in your team that would prove valuable for one of those upcoming audit engagements? Examples may include: a. You are auditing a subsidiary in another country or a third-party vendor in another country, and you need language skills, that is, someone who can speak, read and write in that language. What is also equally important is someone who understands the culture and business ways of working in that country. b. You are performing an audit in an area that requires deep subject matter expertize, perhaps in R&D, quality assurance, legal, sales, manufacturing, information security, etc.

Next, you need to have a think about people you know across your organization, if there is anyone who has those skills that you are looking for and may be looking for a development opportunity to try their hand at auditing. This is where your extensive knowledge of your business and your network comes into play. You may already have some individuals in mind that you know are interested in what Internal Audit does, and so would make excellent candidates.

You will need the buy-in of not only them but also their line manager and their wider department. Typically, a guest auditor rotation could be anywhere from one week to four weeks. This means taking someone out of their day job for a period of time, which their line manager may not be keen on. This is where you need to be able to pitch it well. It is a development opportunity for that individual, and a chance for them to learn new skills, network and build connections. It can enhance their abilities once they are back in their day job, and they can share that experience with their team.

Once you have agreed on a guest auditor, what audit engagement they are going to support you with and agreed timing, the next step is a rapid onboarding exercise. You will need to explain the Internal Audit to your guest auditor and then provide a basic level of training in terms of what you will have them do on the audit. Will they help with the planning, fieldwork, report writing or all of these elements of the audit process? They will need support during their time with you, and that means one of your team members managing and coaching them closely. Do not let them loose on your audit clients without supervision. You must clearly define their roles and responsibilities during the process. Afterwards, you will need to spend time with them to debrief them and ensure they have found it to be a useful experience. Ask them for honest, but constructive, feedback and use that feedback to improve the process next time you use a guest auditor. Keep that relationship and new connection active after they return to their day job. Finally, demonstrate the value it has brought, not only to your audit output but also to that individual, and to your senior management, so that they buy into the idea.

I have had guest auditors that have come from a wide variety of functions, including Corporate Compliance, Legal, Finance, IT,

Quality Assurance and Information Security. On the whole, it has been a fun and fulfilling experience for both parties.

Once you have successfully utilized a couple of guest auditors and had (hopefully) positive feedback from the experience, you can consider initiating a guest auditor program. This can eventually become an embedded process that supplements your function's resource, but more importantly, enhances your output and the value you deliver to the business.

It will bring three tangible and highly visible benefits:

1. Enhanced audit quality and output
2. Foster cross-functional collaboration and
3. Develop talent in your organization.

Those last two will be seen as an unexpected, but pleasant output that many would not expect coming from an Internal Audit function.

4.5.2 Secondments

Think guest auditor, but for a longer period of time. A secondment is a temporary transfer of an employee from their regular role to a different position and department. You can be seconded to an external organization, but in this case, we are talking about someone being seconded from a department in your organization to your Internal Audit function. This is usually for a period that can be anywhere from three to 12 months. Most of the steps discussed above regarding guest auditors apply here. Some broader thinking is required, as you are not just looking at having them work on one specific audit engagement but on several audit engagements during their time with you, and also all the other activities that go with being an internal auditor. Cost-wise it will be different too. With a guest auditor, given the short period of time, there is usually no cost implication. But with a secondment, it is likely that the secondees' cost will hit your cost centre. As this person is already an employee in your organization, there is no additional cost to the business – it is a sunk cost – but there is an impact on your budget. More thought and time are required on your part regarding onboarding, training and development of that person whilst they are working for you. But done successfully, the benefits are the same as with a guest auditor.

4.5.3 Micro-Placements

A micro-placement is a short-term work experience opportunity, typically lasting four to eight weeks, designed to give university students practical exposure to a specific profession or industry. With a little research into local universities in your area, you may well find that they offer their students micro-placements and that they are looking for local businesses to get involved. Getting a university student interested in an opportunity of an Internal Audit role might sound like a tough ask, but it is your responsibility to sell it. Now you may work in an exciting industry or a big brand company, which means students are naturally attracted to joining you whatever the role may be. But if not, you will need to work at this. There is a small cost involved here; nobody should work for free. But given the short period of time, the cost should be manageable to swallow. Similar to the guest auditor, it is likely that the student works on a specific project or audit engagement, and so planning and timing will be key. Unlike a guest auditor or secondment, the student will be new to your organization too, and so there is additional work needed to onboard and manage them. But if you can make it work, there can be great benefits for you and your business. It will give you a fresh perspective and hopefully some innovative ideas that students can bring to help enhance your audit process. It supports the talent pipeline; your business can identify future employees and build a talent pipeline by nurturing those relationships with local universities. And not just a pipeline into Internal Audit, it could be finance, tech, corporate governance, etc. Another great example of something no one expected the Internal Audit function to do.

I'd like to think that accomplishing these three ideas could result in you making a real impact in creating a new generation of internal auditors in your organization!

4.6 Building Resilience and Continuity into Your Internal Audit Function

If you are a one-person Internal Audit function, building resilience and continuity can be a challenge. Some people use the analogy of "what if you were hit by a bus." I am not a fan of this idea; buses are so infrequent these days, the likelihood is so remote. I prefer to think about what if you win the lottery on Friday and decide not to return to work on Monday. What happens to your organization's Internal Audit function? Is it back to square one or is there a continuity plan in place? This is something that you need to think about and plan ahead for. But not only you, this needs the involvement and agreement of your Audit Committee.

Here are three ideas that will help ensure there is some level of resilience in place.

4.6.1 Co-Source

If you have an established co-source partner in place, then this can act as the continuity of your Internal Audit activity. At least on an interim basis. The co-source can continue to work on delivering the Internal Audit engagements in accordance with the agreed audit plan, and they can appoint someone from their firm to act as an interim Head of Internal Audit. This can work well, but the danger is that management chooses to stick with that fully outsourced model. Now I am not saying there is anything wrong with a fully outsourced model, but my preference is always to have at least one person in-house. So, this should be an interim solution until a new CAE can be hired.

4.6.2 Succession Planning

Hopefully, talent development and succession planning are something that you have been working on as a CAE. You will very likely have performed a HR Internal Audit and audited your organization's talent development and succession planning processes; so, no excuses for not practising what you preach. If you have a small in-house team, you may have already identified a potential suitable candidate and have been working on developing them to succeed you. Or you may have identified someone in your organization who works in a different department. Remember, the Internal Audit function is often one of those departments that people move in and out of quite fluidly. I have seen people from Corporate Compliance, Risk Management and Finance move sideways into a CAE position, and this can work very well, and bring new energy and a fresh perspective. Succession planning should also involve looking outside of your organization. Keeping up with the rising superstars in the Internal Audit world, via your network or business social media apps, is an important tool to use. You need to think wider than just your organization, especially if you are working in a small to medium-sized business.

4.6.3 Processes, Documentation and Systemization

Systemizing everything you do in your successful Internal Audit activity means that if, for any reason, you as the CAE is out of the business for a period of time, or has left the business altogether, then your remaining team can continue what they are working on by following the system that you have put in place. Audit engagements can continue to be performed and delivered, and papers for reporting to the Audit Committee can be prepared. Assurance will continue to be provided. This will hopefully work for a period of time long enough for a new CAE to be hired. If there are no systems, processes or templates then it means work will grind to a halt, as the team will lack direction and quality of work will drop.

The lesson here is to learn not to reinvent the wheel when your organization has a gap in Internal Audit activity.

4.6.4 Summary

There is a large selection of ideas and techniques to consider adopting in this chapter. Start with the ideas that resonate the most with you, and those that you think will give you the best ROI. This could be creating an Internal Audit manual right at the start or focusing on creating those key templates that are customer-facing; that is, communications to clients, audit reports or picking out certain AI hacks that could save you time and improve the quality of your work.

Do not overwhelm yourself by trying too much at once. Build on each technique; if it works for you – great, if not – move on to the next. Innovate and invent your own ideas and techniques. Get ahead of the technology curve.

Be methodical, be systematic, be creative.

5
When the CAE is not Just the CAE

Taking on Other Roles

LEARNING OBJECTIVE

The reader will gain an understanding of the implications of taking on other roles, such as Risk Management, in addition to managing a lean Internal Audit function. They will gain an appreciation of how to manage risks around independence and objectivity. They will also understand what can realistically be achieved and how to gain the maximum impact with a light-touch approach.

5.1 Taking on Other Roles

When is a CAE not a CAE? When they are also the Head of Risk Management, the Head of Business Continuity, the Head of Insurance, the Counter-Fraud Specialist and the Head of Sarbanes-Oxley (SOX) Compliance. Many CAEs in smaller organizations will recognize this scenario, where the CAE is just one hat that they wear. In reality, they have multiple roles and responsibilities. These extra-curricular roles may have been in place since they started their role as CAE, or they may have been added to their role over time.

In an ideal world, the CAE is just that – the CAE. This ensures that we can comfortably comply with GIAS standard 7.1 Organizational Independence, which states that:

> The chief audit executive must confirm to the board the organizational independence of the internal audit function at least annually.

DOI: 10.1201/9781003519256-5

Alas, we do not live in an ideal world. Many CAEs, especially in small to medium-sized organisations and in the not-for-profit world and public sector, would find that they have to take on additional roles on top of the CAE role. The most common role by far that I have found is being Head of Internal Audit and Head of Risk. This may form various titles such as Head of Risk Management and Head of Enterprise Risk Management (ERM). Management often considers there to be a natural fit between Risk Management and Internal Audit, and hence, when there is an opportunity to have these as two distinct roles or two distinct functions, more often than not, they are combined. I have also seen where the CAE has taken on the role of being responsible for business continuity in an organisation, and again, management often sees this as a natural fit when considering Internal Audit's role of safeguarding the organisation and providing assurance, that business continuity could potentially fall into that remit. Responsibility for insurance matters can also be seen as a natural fit alongside Internal Audit, and therefore, a CAE may find themselves responsible for managing insurance matters at their organisation. This, perhaps, is best placed in the Corporate Compliance or Procurement functions where possible. And for those organisations that are publicly listed, or newly publicly listed, in the United States, they will need to adhere to the Sarbanes-Oxley Act (SOX), and if there is already an Internal Audit function in place, management may well consider that this existing function can take on the additional responsibilities of ensuring compliance with SOX. Now in larger organisations, it's common to have a separate function responsible for SOX compliance or at least a distinct subset of the Internal Audit function that is responsible for SOX compliance, again to be able to demonstrate the independence and objectivity that Internal Audit should have.

I have had the pleasure of being responsible for Internal Audit and SOX compliance in an organisation, for Internal Audit and Risk Management in another organisation and for Internal Audit and Counter-Fraud in another organisation.

In fact, there has only been one occasion in my career where my sole responsibility was in Internal Audit.

5.2 Maintaining Independence and Objectivity

The question then comes to mind of how we square the circle in being able to ensure independence as an Internal Audit function, whilst we have other business process roles that we are also responsible for. Now, if we have a small team, there is some opportunity to farm out some of those responsibilities to individual team members. But if our Internal Audit function is simply a team of one person, this creates a conundrum.

Thankfully, the new GIAS are on hand to provide some guidance regarding this matter. Let us again refer to GIAS standard 7.1.

> When the chief audit executive has one or more ongoing roles beyond internal auditing, the responsibilities, nature of work, and established safeguards must be documented in the internal audit charter. If those areas of responsibility are subject to internal auditing, alternative processes to obtain assurance must be established, such as contracting with an objective, competent external assurance provider that reports independently to the board.
>
> When the chief audit executive's non-audit responsibilities are temporary, assurance for those areas must be provided by an independent third party during the temporary assignment and for the subsequent 12 months. Also, the chief audit executive must establish a plan to transition those responsibilities to management.
>
> If the governing structure does not support organizational independence, the chief audit executive must document the characteristics of the governing structure limiting independence and any safeguards that may be employed to achieve this principle.

Here, the standards provide a path forward. The first thing that we need to do is think about those additional responsibilities that we have, and the nature of work involved when executing those responsibilities. We then need to think about how we can establish safeguards to be able to maintain our independence. Maintaining our independence is critical, as without it, senior management and the board will have a hard time placing reliance on any assurance that we provide, knowing full well that there is a conflict, especially if we attempt to audit areas and provide assurance on those areas that we are also responsible for.

Let's think about what safeguards we can put in place. As always, as a small Internal Audit function, we need to think about pragmatic practical safeguards that we can realistically put in place that will be effective enough to give assurance to senior management and the Audit Committee/Board of our continued independence.

The obvious one is, of course, that we don't perform any assurance engagements on functions that we are responsible for. If you are the CAE and the Head of Risk Management, you cannot perform an audit engagement on the effectiveness of the organization's Risk Management function. This is a clear case of marking your own homework. And no one will take you seriously. But there is an opportunity to use a third party that is external to the organization to provide an independent review of Risk Management. Again, there are risks here if we are the ones selecting the third party to perform the engagement and we're the ones gatekeeping and issuing the final product of the engagement. We may wish to consider having an alternative function, for example, Corporate Compliance or Legal or ideally, the Audit Committee itself, identifying and engaging with a third party to agree the scope, the audit methodology and the output and ensure that the work is supervised by someone in the organisation other than the CAE, and the output is delivered directly to the Audit Committee. The Internal Audit function will, of course, have to input into the process as they will be the very people that are being audited, that is, the client. Therefore, they will be involved in the planning, field work and end product, but sitting on the other side of the table as the client as opposed to the auditor. They will need to agree with any findings and provide management action plans with responsible owners and appropriate timelines. If the decision is made to not use a third party to conduct this type of review, then in certain organisations, there may be an opportunity for another function that, of course, has the requisite skills to perform an Internal Audit but also the knowledge of Risk Management to perform the work. This approach can be used not just for auditing Risk Management but for any other area that a CAE may have responsibility for; for example, Business Continuity, Insurance, etc.

Whatever safeguards we identify, we need to document these in our Internal Audit Charter, and that updated Charter must then be reviewed and approved by the Audit Committee to demonstrate their agreement with those safeguards. It is good practice to review and update, where necessary, your Internal Audit Charter on an annual basis. If, for any reason during the course of the year, you are required to take on additional responsibilities that impact or potentially impact your independence as CAE, you should look to incorporate this into the Internal Audit Charter and gain approval from the Audit Committee as soon as possible.

The standards also talk about occasions where the CAE may take on additional responsibilities on a temporary basis. A pertinent example of this, where many CAEs found themselves taking on additional roles, was during the 2020 global COVID pandemic. Many organizations chose to defer audit engagements or completely stop the execution of the approved Internal Audit plan due to the impact of the pandemic on the organization. Many CAEs found themselves taking on additional roles and responsibilities at short notice, and their team members were being asked to contribute to business operations. Those with a finance background may have found themselves taking on specific roles in the Finance function when people were unwell or unable to perform tasks required. Many took on additional work and responsibilities around business continuity, given the risks being faced by all organisations due to the pandemic. I had even heard of stories where auditors in retail organisations were asked to take on roles on the ground in fully operational roles outside of their skill set and experience, for example, working in warehouses, driving vehicles, stacking shelves! It was all hands on deck; whatever urgent tasks were required, people from across the organization were asked to chip in, regardless of what their role was supposed to be. It was all about survival for the organization, but also survival for their people – literally – and the people they serve.

Once organizations, and the world, returned to some resemblance of normality, those additional roles and responsibilities that the CAE and auditors had were removed, and they returned to their day jobs. The standards are clear here that where those individuals had responsibility for certain functions and processes and controls, those same individuals could not audit them for a 12-month period. If an audit engagement was required within that 12-month period, an independent party would be required to perform that work. In some instances, those additional responsibilities were not removed and instead became business as usual and an additional responsibility for the CAE.

The optimal scenario, and one that large organizations often have the luxury of, is that the CAE is just that – the Chief Audit Executive, responsible for the Internal Audit function. Nothing more, nothing less. The reality is very different as I have found in my career, and no doubt many of you will have also found.

If you come across a situation where you are being asked to take on additional roles and responsibilities, or you have the inkling and business intel that it may be coming sooner rather than later based on changes that have happened in your organization, then the first step is to push back and state the importance and the fundamental principles of independence and objectivity of the Internal Audit function for it to be able to provide the value that it has done to date. It is quite possible that management either does not realize or has forgotten this fundamental requirement. A simple reminder may be enough for them to realize that providing additional responsibilities will (a) impact independence and (b) impact the quality and quantity of assurance that they are receiving from the function at present. If this is not enough to state your case, and management is continuing to push ahead, then the next step would be to refer them to the standards that state the requirement for independence. The risk here is, of course, that the standards do state that additional responsibilities can be taken on if appropriate safeguards are in place. Next, take your case to the Audit Committee, who should be your strongest supporters and advocates for ensuring independence and objectivity, as they are the key customers placing reliance upon the work that you do.

However, the reality of the situation is that you may well find yourself taking on these additional responsibilities, and management and the Board will look to you to identify, document and implement those safeguards. Once you have taken on those additional responsibilities, there is a real need for clarity, both for yourself to be crystal clear on the different hats you're wearing, and when you are wearing them, and clarity for management, the Board, the stakeholders and, in fact, all the people of the organisation so that they have clarity on the interactions they have with you and which hat you may be wearing at that time.

5.3 Light Touch, Maximum Impact

Let's assume that we are running a best-in-class, effective and efficient, albeit small, Internal Audit function. Senior management, the Board, and our clients are super happy with the work that we are performing and the assurance that we are providing the organisation. But we are at full capacity to be able to achieve this with a small team. Taking on additional roles and responsibilities without being able to increase headcount or increase budget is going to be a tall order. This whole book has been about impact. Making a BIG IMPACT!

Let's see how we can achieve just that, but taking a light-touch approach. We need to think about what we can deliver, what we can achieve, without compromising our already incredible best-in-class Internal Audit function. Whilst the aim is to make maximum impact, the other aim is to, in time, pass on the torch of these extra roles and responsibilities to a new or different function and give them the building blocks and blueprint to deliver what we have done, but on a broader scale.

Let's take what I believe to be the most common example, which is where an individual or a small function is responsible for both delivering Internal Audit and delivering Risk Management. These are two distinct functions that have very different objectives, customers, processes and end products. It is essential not to mix the two up.

Grab a blank piece of paper and draw a line down the middle; on the left is Internal Audit, on the right is Risk Management. Go through this step by step, thinking about the purpose of each function, the customers of each function, the process, the methodology, the end products and the best practice. Looking down at that piece of paper, it should start to become clear how very different these two functions are. Risk Management is a second-line function, and Internal Audit is a third-line function, with different reporting lines. We have just blurred the three-line model that we have all been relying on for years.

The trick is to start Risk Management from scratch, without really starting from scratch. Do not reinvent the wheel; use all the tools, techniques, experience and budget that you have in your arsenal to deliver.

Some options to think about are:

- Getting your co-source to support you
- Sourcing a fixed-term contractor for a short period of time to get Risk Management up and running
- Look inside your organisation for existing expertize and see if you can second someone. A great development opportunity for them!
- Maximize the use of AI, especially LLMs, to help you create the basic building blocks

Decide on a Risk Management methodology; for example, COSO, ISO31000, etc. If you work for a publicly listed company, consider COSO. If you work in manufacturing and your business focuses on adherence and certification to ISO standards, for example, 9001, 27001, 45001, etc., then opt for ISO31000. They all work, so read up about them and select the one you think will best resonate with your business. Then run with it.

Write a Risk Management policy. Many companies publish their Risk Management policy on the internet, and there are many Risk Management policy templates available. You may even consider having an AI LLM do a fair bit of the heavy lifting for you with regards to the content. Then tailor it to align with your business.

Nothing has to be perfect. It has to be fit for purpose and enough to get by, with the aim of updating and enhancing with future iterations. If you are working towards perfection, you will never get anything done.

Think ahead to the output. What does your C-suite and your broader senior management team really want to get out of Risk Management? Find this out through robust conversations with them. Is it to tick a box for regulatory requirements? Is it because the parent company are demanding it? Is it because management wants to get a greater understanding of the risks the business faces to help drive its strategy and goals? Are they worried about blind spots in the risk landscape that they are not seeing? Does the C-suite want to instil a culture of active Risk Management and accountability across the middle levels of the business?

Once you know the answer to this question, you can then identify what output is required and work back from that to deliver exactly what management is after. With that clear line of sight, you can remove numerous activities and work streams that would otherwise have slowed down your progress.

Ideas for the output that will delight your customers are, of course, based on the answers to the questions above. But some ideas that could work include:

- A visually impactful risk-reporting dashboard – think Power BI or Tableau-driven, with access given to people to be able to dip into at any point and get real-time status information.
- Easy-to-use, system-based risk registers to disseminate across the business for them to own and use. No Excel spreadsheets please!
- A Risk Management training course to be deployed across the business. Do not deliver this in person or online again and again. Record the session and use an AI avatar software to translate to multiple languages if required. Keep it short, 15–20 minutes max, just like a TED talk and upload it your electronic Learning Management System so it is available to each and every employee.
- Link the existing business reporting dashboard to your risk dashboard and select the key data drivers to provide a view of risk. Use formats and templates that your leaders are already used to seeing, so it feels familiar to them.
- Deliver Risk Management training to your C-suite and or Audit Committee and Senior Leadership teams. A great way to do this is to have your co-source partner deliver the training, ideally someone at the Director or Partner level with the right level of gravitas. They will have had experience of delivering these training sessions for many of their other clients.

If the business really wants it, then work on risk appetite, risk tolerance, risk velocity and Key Risk Indicators (KRIs). If this is not their priority, then it is not your priority. So, that will come later.

Do not over-promise as management will not thank you for this. Make clear that with this being an additional ask, it will take time. How much time is for you to assess and agree upon, but it is not weeks; it may be months, it may even be anywhere up to 24 months. Throughout the process, reiterate the time it will take, whilst all the while laying the groundwork to make the business case for additional resources for it to work as a fully functioning business-as-usual activity. This will be a second-line function that needs to be outside of the responsibility of the third-line Internal Audit function.

By working on all these areas, using this light-touch approach, you will make significant headway, and hopefully, at the same time, give the customer what they want, which is maximum impact!

6

Building Counter-Fraud Services to an Internal Audit Function

LEARNING OBJECTIVE

The reader will gain an understanding of the best approach to building a Counter-Fraud framework if requested to do so by management or required by regulators. They will gain insights and ideas on how best to use technology to support fraud prevention, detection and deterrence. The reader will also learn how best to approach performing fraud investigations if required to do so, and the risks in taking on investigations.

6.1 Introduction

One of those additional roles that we've just talked about in Chapter 5 could be to lead counter-fraud at your organization or play an active part in supporting counter-fraud. As with any additional role and responsibility, it is essential to be clear right at the start what part you will play. Will this entail communications to raise awareness, performing fraud risk assessments, performing fraud investigations, delivering training, etc? One must bear in mind that as a small Internal Audit shop, your focus should be on delivering a best-in-class Internal Audit function, and therefore, this may not leave adequate time and resources to be able to either lead or support counter-fraud in your organization.

 DOI: 10.1201/9781003519256-6

6.2 Counter-Fraud Framework

However, if this is a task that you do take on, the first thing to consider is the creation of a Counter-Fraud framework. Being able to visualise and map out your Counter-Fraud framework is a great place to start. There's a lot to include, and once you have a view of what you would like your framework to be, only at that point should you begin to unpack and get into the details of how to deliver the framework to support the organization in fighting fraud.

6.2.1 Tone at the Top

The key elements of a Counter-Fraud framework must start with tone at the top coming directly from the Board, executive oversight and buy-in. You will need a Counter-Fraud strategy document that has the agreement of the C-suite, the Board, and, to a certain extent, the next level of senior management that will help support in preventing, detecting and deterring fraud.

6.2.1.1 Internal Control Framework, Policies and Procedures There needs to be a strong internal control framework, and often when we think of internal controls, our focus is on financial controls, but in fact, when it comes to fraud, we need to think about internal controls with regards to activities that take place in functions such as People/Human Resources, Procurement, Sales and Marketing, Information Technology, Information Security, etc. With those internal controls in mind, we should have a layer of policies and procedures which either directly or indirectly support fighting fraud in the organization. These policies and procedures should include:

- Anti-bribery and corruption policy
- Anti-money laundering policy
- Whistle-blowing policy
- Financial control policy or handbook
- Code of conduct and performance
- Conflicts of Interest policy
- Gifts and Hospitality policy
- IT and Information Security policies
- Travel and expenses policy

Other elements would include investigation procedures, fraud response plans and a Fraud Risk Assessment.

6.2.2 Fraud Risk Assessment

Next, we need to think about proactive prevention and proactive detection. The first step is to perform a Fraud Risk Assessment. Have we performed one in the past? When did we last perform it? How detailed was it? Did any actions arise from it? Were they tracked through to implementation?

Performing a Fraud Risk Assessment should be an ongoing activity, conscious that the first time this is done, it will absolutely be a time-consuming exercise. However, if regularly updated and iterated, this activity becomes less cumbersome and ensures that you have an accurate and current view of fraud risk in your organization. If it is not regularly reviewed and updated, and becomes stale, it increases the risk of fraud occurring due to the velocity of change when it comes to new and evolving fraud schemes.

6.2.3 Fraud Response Plan

A fraud response plan is a documented plan of what activities will occur if fraud were to happen in the organization; for example, who needs to be contacted, do we have any templates to help perform an investigation, how do we handle internal and external Comms, who will perform the investigation and how do we report on the outcomes. This plan should be agreed with management and shared with them so that they understand what roles and responsibilities they play in this process.

6.3 Fraud Awareness Training

Delivering fraud awareness training is critical in your organization. Fraud awareness training is not a one-off exercise. This training should be delivered regularly. I would suggest at least annually at all organizations. You should also consider whether a Counter-Fraud module should be included as part of the new employee onboarding at your organization. This could be in the form of a mandatory interactive training session on your company's electronic LMS. There are many off-the-shelf modules that you can find, but it is best to tailor it so that it is specific to your organization – so, either create it in-house or use a reputable company to develop a bespoke module for you. As with all e-learning, keep it short and sweet, but make sure you cover all the relevant topics.

Gary Sommerford (Director at Larus Consulting, a UK-based counter fraud consultancy) offers the following perspective:

> There should be a certain level of fraud awareness training across an organisation, because it's not a Finance thing. It's not a Procurement thing. It could happen anywhere across your entire organization.

It is also important to think about who your audience is. People often fall into the trap of thinking that fraud awareness training should only be delivered to the Finance function. Fraud is all about stealing money after all, right? Well, no, the reality is that fraud can occur anywhere in the organization, and therefore, there is a need for fraud awareness training for all employees, and that includes senior management and the Board. Remember our focus on tone at the top. But it is important to think about the content of the fraud awareness training given to these different audiences. There is a need to have some standard training material that is applicable to all employees, whether they be senior management, finance, HR, operational, sales and marketing, etc. Then there is a need to tailor an element of the training specific to your audience. So, for example, in a Finance Shared Service Centre, where teams are responsible for accounts receivable, accounts payable, treasury, etc., you may wish to focus on fraud schemes, red flags and how to spot those types of frauds that are specific to these processes. And if delivering awareness training to a People/HR function, you may wish to focus on relevant frauds that may impact them around recruitment, qualifications, right to work, interview, references, etc.

One of the comments I have received in the past is "are you not just teaching people how to commit fraud?" My sincere hope is that employees will be able to recognise that what they are being taught are the red flags to look out for and be given the confidence to raise their hand and speak up when they have concerns regarding potential fraud. Yes, there may be a small percentage of the people that you are training who are criminally natured and, therefore, may utilise what you have taught them to attempt to commit fraud in your organization. Hopefully, through the other work that you are doing in the Counter-Fraud space, there will be appropriate internal controls specifically designed to prevent and detect fraud; therefore, those individuals will not be successful in their endeavours. To those potential fraudsters in your organization, the training can act as a deterrent, a warning shot, to let people know that we are aware of the types of fraud that could occur and that we are watching and remaining ever vigilant.

There is a question as to who should provide this fraud awareness training. This may be something that you feel that you are able to deliver yourself, either because you have experience and qualifications in this field; for example, you may be a Certified Fraud Examiner (CFE) or an Accredited Counter-Fraud Specialist (ACFS), and therefore you have the knowledge and expertize to create the training materials and deliver the training yourself.

You also need to weigh up the time, effort and energy required to create the training materials and then deliver this training across your organization on an ongoing basis and whether this is feasible given your current role, responsibilities and workload. Perhaps, there is someone in your team who has the ability, knowledge and experience to deliver the training. In fact, it may well be a development opportunity for them to be able to deliver the training – an opportunity to work on and improve their presentation skills and to build and grow their network by delivering the training to functions across the entire organization.

One option that I have used in a previous role is to have a reputable third-party company prepare and deliver fraud awareness training across the organization. There is obviously a cost to this, and you will have to consider that, given your function's budget, but the big advantage here is that they will be preparing and delivering the training and that they will have the experience, expertize and current knowledge of fraud risks, current fraud schemes and real-life examples of threats to organizations. Given that the third-party will not be a part of your organization and has limited experience or understanding of your organization, it is critical that you work with them to make sure that the training is tailored specifically to your industry, your sector and your unique organization. A lengthy, generic fraud awareness training session that has not been tailored will not land well with your audiences and therefore will not achieve the intended purpose, which is to raise fraud awareness and help people in the organization to recognise potential fraud and speak up. People will not engage, and it will be a missed opportunity. You may wish to have a third-party also help you in preparing an onboarding training module on counter fraud that would then be available for all to access via your organization's electronic Learning Management System.

Once awareness training has been delivered across your entire organization, it's time to start thinking about how this will be delivered on a regular basis. Delivering the same training every year to the same employees will become stale. People will not attend, be disinterested and will not take it seriously. You will not achieve the outcomes that you were hoping for. So, there is a need to refresh, update and adapt the training that you deliver on a regular basis. The world of fraud is rapidly changing; there are new schemes, new techniques and new technology utilized and this is changing every day. Therefore, there is a real need to make sure that whatever training is delivered is up to date and is current and relevant to the time and to your organization. An option here is to mix up your approach to training, where perhaps each year you use a different third-party provider to deliver the training to ensure variety and address a broad range of fraud risks. Or you may also wish to consider a mix of delivering some of this training yourself and some of this using a third party, again to provide training that is tailored and that will land well with your organization, but also includes the most current and relevant content based on expertize from outside the organization. There is no one right way of doing this, but there are numerous options, and it will be your responsibility to work out which one will land best with your employees and will work optimally to keep your organization as safe as possible from the threat of fraud.

Dr Stephen Hill (Counter-Fraud Expert & Founder of Hill Bingham) has a clear message:

> I've heard some organizations saying training is a luxury. It is not a luxury. It is something that you must do.

6.4 Fraud Risk and the Role of the Audit Committee

Your Audit Committee and or Board (depending on the Corporate Governance structure of your organization) has an important role and responsibility when it comes to Fraud Risk Management. The overarching thing your Audit Committee needs is *Assurance* from management and the organization. This assurance should be ongoing, and not just a one-off annual update. The primary goal is to ensure that fraud risk is being actively managed through processes, controls and people.

As discussed earlier in this chapter, the Audit Committee should be placing importance on having a comprehensive Counter-Fraud framework and an annual Counter-Fraud workplan to sit alongside this framework. This Counter-Fraud workplan should include proactive steps and be reported on regularly. A positive way of providing assurance is demonstrating that your organization has relevant policies and procedures in place, such as those listed above. And that these policies are effective, up-to-date and in line with current laws and regulations.

Communication is another critical aspect. There is a need for active communication within the organization to raise awareness about fraud risks. This includes sending out warnings about various types of frauds, such as phishing, payment fraud, payroll fraud and procurement fraud. The effectiveness of these communications should be monitored through metrics like engagement rates and hit rates. This can all be reported to the Audit Committee. Training is of crucial interest. There should be mandatory training sessions, and the frequency and types of training should be tracked. Metrics on the number of people trained and the completion rates of these training sessions are essential for assessing the effectiveness of the training programs.

Being able to track and report on fraud allegations and understanding their trends is key to include in Audit Committee reporting. This reporting should include the number of fraud allegations, with some quarterly trending to give perspective, and industry/sector benchmarking where available. This helps in building a picture of the organization's fraud risk over time.

Investigation status is another key area to report on. Your Audit Committee should be informed, on a quarterly basis, about the status of ongoing investigations, including the number of investigations launched, ongoing and closed. The outcomes of these investigations and the severity of the frauds being investigated should also be reported.

Understanding the dynamics of criminal and civil prosecutions can be helpful to incorporate. While criminal prosecutions may be less common, especially in certain geographies, civil prosecutions are often pursued to reclaim funds. The success rates of these prosecutions and the amounts recovered are important metrics to track.

The actual amount of money lost to fraud is another critical metric. Your Audit Committee members will want to know the exact amounts lost to fraud and how much the organization could have lost had the fraud not been detected. This helps in assessing the effectiveness of the Counter-Fraud work plan and the adequacy of the processes and controls in place.

It is important to emphasize the need to gain support from your Audit Committee when it comes to the Counter-Fraud effort. Fraud risk should be explained to the Audit Committee members, and bespoke training sessions should be provided to upskill them. Regular discussions with the Chair of the Audit Committee and other members are also recommended to ensure that fraud risk is given the necessary attention. Depending on the country and organization's legal structure, there may also be legal duties and responsibilities that the Board and company directors are liable for. Emphasizing this can be a great way to focus the minds of the people at the top. I am pretty sure none of your Board members want to find themselves in a jail cell because they did not have adequate procedures and controls in place to prevent fraud.

The key message here is the need for ongoing assurance, effective communication, regular training and thorough tracking of fraud allegations and investigations. By following these practices, the Audit Committee members can gain the assurance that they are seeking, that fraud risk is being actively managed and mitigated.

Gary Sommerford's thoughts on this are:

> Your Board or Audit Committee enerally don't want the detail – keep it high-level. But they do want to know how long that fraud is going on? How much has it cost us? And then, dependent on the type and nature of that fraud, you look at generally 12 months in the future. Had this fraud

not been stopped, how much money would we have lost over the next 12-month period? What is the trending on numbers of fraud allegations coming through, and are we investigating them in a timely manner?

6.5 Focus on Fraud Awareness

When we consider ways to prevent, detect and deter fraud, how best to do this often starts with an organization's culture. To develop a culture of fraud awareness and confidence in speaking up when red flags are spotted, there are a number of steps that we can take.

What businesses will tell you, again and again, is that they are really busy with – and then will reel off a long list of tasks and activities. Getting people's attention to talk to them about Counter-Fraud can be a challenge. So, to raise awareness and develop that culture that we talked about, you are going to need to use a number of methods and try and be innovative in your approach. If one approach is not yielding the results you hoped for, then you need to pivot.

Examples of actions that you can take to raise fraud awareness could include:

- Creating and circulating newsletters on Counter-Fraud
- Regular comms via emails sent companywide with clear messaging, recent cases – internal or external
- Comms via any internal social media platforms your organization uses
- Create and put up posters in locations people are likely to see them, that is, breakout areas, next to the coffee machine, in the bathrooms!
- Get IT to set up screensavers on company laptops, so when people lock their screens, the screensaver is a Counter-Fraud message
- Set up a table outside the staff cafeteria and spread the word, create and hand out leaflets
- Hold in-person or online drop-in sessions, where people can ask you questions to find out more
- Use events such as "International Fraud Awareness Week" to promote fraud awareness using the tools and materials that are provided with this and other similar events

Often, it is simply about getting out and speaking to people face to face and outside of formal meetings. Offer to join people's team meetings and have a 10–15-minute slot to talk about fraud risk, ensuring that you tailor it to be specific about that team or function.

Dr Hill's thoughts on this are:

> Training is imperative from the bottom right the way to the top of your organization. But I also believe training isn't good enough on its own. I would advocate for continuous on-the-job reminders. An example of this could be reminders at team meetings. Particularly if there's a new fraud risk that's been identified through an audit, investigation or recent case at another company.

6.6 Performing Fraud Investigations

Similarly to the question we posed earlier about who should provide fraud awareness training is the question of who should perform fraud investigations when required. Perhaps you feel confident enough to perform an investigation yourself, especially if you have the requisite experience and qualifications (CFE, ACFS) in this field.

It is entirely feasible that CFE or not, as a qualified internal auditor, you may be fully capable of performing an internal fraud investigation for low-level fraud; for example, minor expenses fraud or supplier invoicing fraud. We have to ask ourselves the same question: given that this is not our primary role, are we taking away valuable resources from focusing on the work of the Internal Audit function and the delivery of the independent and objective assurance activities that our customers require from us? Depending on the type and scale of the fraud allegation, an investigation could be very labour intensive. It could require travel, potentially to other countries and jurisdictions that might put you or your team in danger.

What has undoubtedly changed in the last few years is the complexity of fraud schemes we now see in the current environment. Technology-enabled fraud schemes are not to be taken lightly. Let's be honest, almost all fraud now is being facilitated and aided by some sort of technology.

The purpose of this chapter is not to provide extensive detail on how to perform a fraud investigation. There are much better sources for you to learn about this. There are clear methodologies and procedures required to perform fraud investigations, and these need to be followed to ensure there is a chance of success.

These steps typically involve:

- Assembling a team of professionals with the right skillsets
- Defining the scope of the investigation, based on the allegation
- Preserving the evidence
- Conducting interviews – employees, witnesses and suspects
- Analysing financial records, documentation and any other evidence
- Obtaining advice from legal professionals
- Documenting your findings
- Writing up your investigation report
- Making recommendations to implement future preventative measures

That's quite a long list of steps, and a lot of work for one person, or a small team to accomplish.

The biggest risk you take on here is getting it wrong. What if you miss something because you simply do not have the experience or expertize to perform forensic investigations? Do you really have the skillset as an internal auditor to seize laptops, obtain all the data stored on them and interrogate it? Do you have the skills to perform fraud investigation interviews; these are very different to performing walkthrough meetings on an Internal Audit.

On your own, you cannot do what a team of highly skilled investigators does in a reputable Counter-Fraud consultancy. If you miss something or make a wrong move, you risk the fraudster getting away because they have been tipped off – investigations can be time critical. Evidence could be lost or destroyed. All this can impact the ability to achieve a criminal prosecution.

There is a balance to be had here. When triaging a fraud allegation, you may wish to consider what the size of the fraud is likely to be and the risk to the business. You do have to weigh up the cost of using a third-party to perform the investigation versus doing it yourself. And fraud investigations can be costly.

What may seem at first to be a small-scale, simple fraud scheme could be huge. It could have a significant financial risk and or reputational risk to your business. Put it this way; if in a few years' time this huge fraud ends up being part of a public inquiry, and you face intense questioning and scrutiny from the government – and it is being televised live – are you going to be comfortable saying that you thought you could handle the investigation by yourself, and you didn't see the need for a specialist fraud investigation firm, and besides, they would have cost too much.

Dr Hill has a firm view when it comes to performing investigations:

> My key advice here is: if you're not experienced to deal with it, DON'T deal with it. You should bring someone in that has the experience. So that would either be law enforcement, noting that some organizations do not want to bring in the police because they don't want it to go public, which it will do through law enforcement; or you bring in a reputable third-party organization that has the expertise to perform that investigation. And this is critical when it comes to certain types of fraud e.g. involving complex technology, ransomware, cyber-attacks, etc. I've known too many that think they can deal with this but end up putting their organizations at more risk from the cost and reputational standpoint.

6.7 The Final Word on Fraud

Gary Sommerford has a saying that, whether we are acting in a Counter-Fraud capacity or in our Internal Audit roles, we should always seek fine grain detail and consider:

> The ABC of fraud: Assume nothing. Believe nothing, Check everything! This mnemonic is a guiding principle for investigators to maintain a critical and objective mindset by avoiding assumptions, suspending belief until evidence is verified, and systematically challenging all information to ensure accuracy and reliability.

7
Impactful Products That Drive Change

LEARNING OBJECTIVE

The reader will gain an appreciation of the importance of branding their Internal Audit function and ideas on how best to market the function to key stakeholders and their wider organization. They will obtain valuable insights and practical ideas of how to make their outputs and end products appealing, engaging and valuable to their clients. The chapter will provide ideas on how to work towards becoming a trusted advisor and how to impress your Audit Committee with what you're able to produce and the value that you can bring on a limited budget.

7.1 Introduction

All of what we have talked about in the previous six chapters will be of little value if we cannot produce end products that make an impact.

I do believe that it is essential to think of yourself and your Internal Audit function as a business. Take a step back and imagine that your Internal Audit function is a business that offers its customers products and services. What is your product – assurance, insight, foresight, advice to improve the organization you work for, safeguard the organization and help it achieve its goals and strategy? What form does your product take – traditionally, this has been lengthy written audit reports and presentations to your Audit Committee, Board and C-suite. Much of this still holds true, but your product output needs to be much broader, more innovative and tailored to your customer base. We have already discussed the requirement per the new

DOI: 10.1201/9781003519256-7

standards to communicate our results, which does not always require the traditional written audit report. There is a need to think about what your customer really wants, how they want it and when they want it.

Think about product quality, but also build in customer service, features, benefits and brand reputation. All these elements are essential for the future of your Internal Audit activity.

7.2 Branding and Marketing Your Internal Audit Function

Now that you are clear on your products and your customers, it is time to think about branding and marketing your Internal Audit function.

Seek out support from the brand teams, sales and marketing teams and Comms teams in your organizations. They will have expertize in this area and can provide useful guidance and advice. Do your market research. Working through your list of customers, that is, Board, C-suite, mid-management, shareholders, local communities you operate in, etc. try to gain an understanding of what they want from you and in what format.

Raise awareness across your organization, and at all levels and locations. Create presentations, "an introduction to your Internal Audit team." Try different formats; these could be online sessions, face-to-face lunch and learn sessions, a pre-recorded short video, maybe with some animation, an intranet site, a regular blog/vlog, your organization's social media platforms, etc.

Think about the branding of your function, and aim to get a consistent look for all end products, reports, presentations, emails, comms, intranet and social media posts, posters, etc. Consider the use of a logo and consider a tag line. Or you may decide that these are not necessary or will not work with your customer base.

7.3 Engaging with Your Clients

You need an Internal Audit Customer Relationship Management (CRM) system. All successful businesses will have a CRM system to manage and drive positive relationships with their clients. Continuing to think of your Internal Audit function as a business, you should also create and actively manage a CRM system to help drive customer engagement. Do not go investing in a Salesforce or ServiceNow system; keep it simple, perhaps a spreadsheet or Microsoft List.

Identify and list out all your customers. These will include Board members, C-suite, Non-Executive Directors (NEDs), mid-management, shareholders, external auditors and other assurance functions. This will be an active database that will change over time, so you will find that you will need to add/remove/edit customers. For each customer, include details such as their roles, experience, preferences, audit output, communication history, interests, specific needs or requirements they have expressed and any other relevant notes. Do not overcomplicate this database by adding too many fields. It will become too unwieldy, and you will find that you will not actively keep it updated. Have a communication strategy and plan for each customer, for example, how often you should interact with them, preferred medium (face to face, online, email, etc.).

By taking this approach, you will greatly improve communication and collaboration with your key customers. You create a personalized approach bespoke to your customers, aligned to their needs and preferences. This enhances your engagement with your customers, their perception of you and the value you bring to them over time.

7.4 Innovative Outputs

How do we make our end products innovative? Let's stop to think about what we want our customers to get out of our products, and how to keep them coming back for more.

We have covered a lot of ground already in Chapter 4 on standardizing processes, using technology and AI tools to innovate when it comes to those end products.

I will offer a few more ideas as food for thought on pushing even further with ways to delight your customers.

7.4.1 Translating Audit Reports

If there is a need to translate your audit reports into another language, doing this manually is now a thing of the past. Why not consider building on the video Internal Audit report idea and have an avatar deliver that Internal Audit report? And most helpfully, you can use software that will deliver that very same Internal Audit report in various languages. When I worked for a Japanese pharmaceutical company, each regional audit function would produce its audit reports in its local language – for us in the United Kingdom and our American colleagues, that was in English. For our Chinese colleagues, their reports would be in Mandarin. But our Japanese Head Office would require the final report in English and Japanese. That means a member of our Japan audit team would have to spend a significant amount of time translating the audit reports written in English to Japanese and the audit reports written in Mandarin to English *and* Japanese. Imagine if there was a way to do that instantly! Well, there is. And it is available on the market right now. Sure, some human intervention is still required; you would want to proofread and quality control the translated report to ensure it delivers the same message.

Let us now think of this the other way around. You are performing an Internal Audit in a non-English speaking country, and you have written your audit report in English, which may well be super helpful for Head Office and the Board, but far less helpful for your clients in the country where the actions need to be implemented. Translate the report you have just issued from English to the relevant local language, and hopefully, you will get a much more positive response, given this extra step you have taken to help them understand your findings and understand the actions they need to take to reduce risk.

7.4.2 Recording Meetings

Record your audit engagement closing meeting. Start the transcription functionality. Use the transcription to support you in drafting relevant sections of the report. If you have explained each finding and then discussed and gained alignment on the corresponding management action, action owner and timing for completion, then use the transcript and some good prompting to have the LLM create these sections of your audit report.

Recording other meetings during an audit engagement, for example, process walk-throughs, planning interviews, status meetings, and then obtaining a summary of the meeting, including actions to share with attendees, can be a great output for the clients you are directly auditing.

7.4.3 Imagery

Reach out to your Corporate Comms team and obtain stock images of your organization to build into the audit reports to make them more visual and draw the attention of the reader. These can be general images, for example, of your company's offices, products or people. Or these can be more specific based on the audit scope you are reporting on. You can even take your own images to include in the report. Images on the front and back of the report and throughout can make a very plain text-heavy traditional audit report into a glossy, visually impactful product that someone wants to pick up and read.

7.4.4 The Two-Page Executive Summary

If you need to stick to, for now at least, a written Internal Audit report, aim to create a two-page Executive Summary. Yes, I said two-page. I am not against the one-page Executive Summary. If you find a good template that works for you, go for it! But I have often found there is not enough white space, and it creates a crowded, unsightly page that I struggle to want to read. Remember, no one (I hope) is actually going to physically print out your audit report or executive summaries – if they do still print out audit reports, you have my permission to shout at them! So, a two-page Executive Summary is not really two pages anymore because your reader is looking at it on a laptop, tablet or phone. That means, using their fingertips, they can make the text and visuals in the report as small or large as they wish, and they can swipe from side to side and up and down to help them navigate to what they want to focus on. Keep the format consistent so that whenever they read your Executive Summary, regardless of which report it is, they know where to find the sections that they are most interested in. I am going to want to go straight away to the overall report rating, but then I also want to see the scope, see the number of findings and see if management has agreed with the actions. Because I am familiar with the layout and design, I can do this quickly and confidently. Ensure you have some impactful data visualizations to provide some of the context and detail in a non-text format. I should be able to read and absorb the Executive Summary in around two minutes and read in detail a little more if the report peaks my interest. And that's it. In five minutes – absolute maximum – I have digested your Executive Summary, including relevant detailed findings, and already created thoughts in my mind of any follow-up questions, concerns or how I am going to act upon what I have read.

If you can't get your Executive Summary down to two pages, then try harder! Because your Audit Committee Chair – your key customer – may insist on that one-pager!

Hunada Nouss OBE (Non-Executive Director, Chair of Audit & Risk Committee, former CFO, COO) offers her view:

> If there's an audit report that we need to see, I'd like to see it as an 'audit on a page'. If somebody wants to read the full report, they can do. But what I want is a sense of why we audited this, what was covered, what the key issues were, is there anything we -as the audit committee or management - need to worry about?

7.4.5 The Humble Email

How about having the humble email replace your audit report or audit memorandum? Email is becoming somewhat old fashioned in day-to-day business communication. So many consider receiving an email akin to receiving a formal letter. Write an email to your clients with the message you wish to convey to them. No audit report, not even an audit memorandum.

This can be extremely valuable when giving real-time assurance at regular points, for say a project assurance engagement. You can have an email template ready so that each regular email communication has the same format and feel. You can use AI to take the first run at creating the email based on your current working papers. The usual caveat applies, which is to never rely on AI, LLMs – or to that end, humans – always review, edit, sense check, and perform quality control before your end product is delivered, in this case, emailed to your clients.

And to go one step further, your output can be a conversation with your client. That is often the best way to communicate your engagement results. If you retain a transcript for your records and for the client to refer to, then that is evidence of communication, and also a tangible product for the client to refer to.

Looking back on all these options for innovative output, how much time have you just saved as a small team by changing your output from lengthy, clunky-written audit reports to emails, conversations or videos? Get good at this, and you will save hours, days or weeks – which gives you more time to focus on all the other activities that really matter.

7.5 Becoming a C-suite Trusted Advisor

The requirements in GIAS Standard 8.1 Board Interaction state that:

> The Chief Audit Executive must provide the board with the information needed to conduct its oversight responsibilities. This information may be specifically requested by the board or may be, in the judgment of the chief audit executive, valuable for the board to exercise its oversight responsibilities.

Simply stated, you must give the Board what they need to allow them to adequately discharge their duties. This is a two-way street. You must give the Board the information they need in the format that they request or prefer. The Board, in turn, must communicate their perspectives and expectations with you.

The buzzwords that we always keep hearing are "becoming a trusted advisor" to the business. But how can you get to this holy grail, and how do you know when you have got there?

Steve Stanbury, Director of Internal Audit at City St George's University emphasizes:

> The importance of being objective, honest, transparent, and impartial can be the key to becoming a trusted advisor to the C-Suite. Trust is earned through delivering high-quality assurance work. These are the key components in building this trust. Never underestimate the importance of professional courage in maintaining trust. Avoiding politics and being open and honest are crucial for a Head of Internal Audit.

7.6 Impressing the Board and Audit Committee

I thought the best way of explaining how to impress your Audit Committee Chair and Committee Members was to simply ask a selection of Audit Committee members and chairs what they want from their CAEs.

Here is what they told me:

Tanya Coff (Non-Executive Director and former CEO and CFO) explains:

> My vision of an ideal internal audit function would be one that evolves by aligning more closely with the organization's risk management process, focuses on horizon scanning, and is recognized as a valued partner by the wider business. It must be proactive and forward-looking rather than reactive. You should be actively breaking down silos and ensuring transparency and awareness of issues to help us manage business risks effectively.

There are high expectations from Audit Committees, including being able to demonstrate specialized knowledge and skills, innovative audit capability and a broader understanding of business risks and business acumen. Alongside this, there must be strong soft skills such as interpersonal and communication skills."

Tanya continues:

> I appreciate audit leaders that are independent thinkers and have the confidence to raise concerns but also commend good practices. These are highly valued traits for a head of internal audit. It is important that they are not influenced by organizational culture and have the courage to call things out as they are.

What is also valued and can help increase your visibility to the Audit Committee is proactively getting involved in advisory work on new business initiatives or ad hoc investigations.

Shahana Khan OBE (Non-Executive Director/CEO/CFO) offers her view: "*I cannot emphasize enough the importance of transparency and honesty in a head of internal audit. They are my 'independent watchdog' and I need them to be open and transparent with me.*"

There is a level of experience that your Audit Committee members will expect and that experience should have allowed you to build up a high level of resilience. One could even look at this as having the wounds and scars from past experience to allow you to stand your ground and not be easily influenced by executives.

Examples of valued work that Heads of Internal Audit can deliver include regular meetings with their Audit Committee chairs, proactive communication with Audit Committee members and the ability to identify and address issues before they escalate.

Scheduling regular check-in meetings with your Audit Committee chair will ensure that they are staying informed about potential risks and issues that you are identifying. The best Heads of Internal Audit will meet with their chairs regularly to discuss risks, issues, pain points and key themes that they are identifying. Audit Committee chairs will appreciate being informed prior to committee meetings and having the comfort that there will be no surprises.

Proactive communication is a value driver as it allows Audit Committee chairs to address issues as they begin to bubble up and before they become significant problems to the business.

Shahana continues: "*The skills I feel are of the utmost importance are knowledge, experience, and the ability to speak out without fear.*"

Internal auditors must have the necessary knowledge and experience to perform their roles effectively. They should be well-versed in their field and capable of delivering valuable insights through the work they perform. Internal auditors must be able to speak out without fear. They should not hide behind others and should be confident in expressing their opinions. There are ways and means to achieve this to ensure maximum impact. And when we talk about impact, it is about how your approach will affect positive change in your organization.

Increasing the visibility of you as the Head of Internal Audit and your Internal Audit team is an important strategy to implement. Increased visibility means more opportunities to impress. In addition to the regular touch-base meetings we discussed, consider holding workshops or information sessions on specific topics to keep your committee current on relevant areas that will help them in their role and support them in understanding the business and or industry. These workshops provide an opportunity for deeper engagement and understanding. Look for opportunities for proactive communication. Reaching out to Audit Committee members outside of scheduled meetings to discuss findings and ensure everyone is on the same page could be an added service that your committee members really value.

Shahana offers the following perspective:

> Examples of actions that demonstrate excellent performance from internal auditors include demonstrating detailed knowledge of their papers, ability to speak in a manner that commands respect and gains the attention of the audit committee. Having the detail to hand and having excellent communication skills will go a long way to the committee trusting their judgment and recommendations.

Hunada Nouss OBE (Non-Executive Director, Chair of Audit & Risk Committee, former CFO, COO) gives her thoughts on her expectations:

> Have a strong enough relationship that you can actually speak truth unto power. You can be respected, but you don't have to be loved. You have to be able to have the strength of relationship that says "look, this is not working, or this is not right or there is a problem here that we need to unpick.
>
> Many people come into audit with strong process operational skills, whereas I think you need strategic insight as well as the operational. I think it's that strategic insight that helps you map the organization, map the assurance and map the compliance culture in an organization.

Hunada continues,

> You can go and do a good few payroll and financial control audits - and core process reviews need to be covered. But it is about stepping back and saying what are the big risks in the organization. Where could I do something a bit different that people haven't seen before.
>
> The thing that sometimes frustrates me is when it feels like an audit plan is going for the easy pickings. You get audits that are all rated as 'Significant Assurance'; and you think, well, are we really looking in the dark corners? Are we really taking on some of the difficult issues in this

organization? So, in a sense it is about an appetite to be curious and have the grit to tackle those areas.

7.7 Writing Board Papers

Writing reports and papers that are destined for the Board or Audit Committee can be a daunting task. Let's consider how best to do that. When you think of your typical Audit Committee pack, it can be 100 pages, which is, in fact, a very concise pack. Poor examples, in my experience, are when you have a pack of 300+ pages. To be honest, no one is really going to sit and read 300+ pages in advance of a committee and be able to take it all in. You will lose interest pretty quickly, and you will not be able to get a feel for what the real issues are that need focus and challenge when it comes to sitting in that boardroom.

You need your paper to standout. You want your paper to be the best paper in the pack. It's not a competition, but it kind of is; so, you want your paper to be better than all the other papers in the pack. My advice would be to aim for two to four pages maximum, with an appendix for supporting documentation. Supporting documentation may include the Executive Summaries of recently issued audit reports and advisory memos, horizon scanning, a dashboard with KPIs and a granular view of the current status of management actions. Your goal should be to make your paper crisp and concise.

Focus on answering the "so what?" question. Think about what you want to tell your Board, and then challenge yourself by asking, "so what?" What does this mean? Why are you telling me this?

Another top tip is "don't tell me everything. Just tell me what I need to know." On too many occasions, I have received an Audit Committee pack, and a paper can be incredibly lengthy because the writer has written down everything that they and their department have done since the last Audit Committee. Three months of granular detail – in the first week of January the team worked on X, in the second week, they began to work on Y and in March they completed Z. It is really great that you and the team have worked so hard over the past three months, and I understand that you want to highlight this to demonstrate how hard you have been grafting, but the Board paper is not the place to state this. Tell me what I need to know. Letting me know, very briefly, your activity during the past three months is fine. But then quickly move on to what that means – what were the results, how was it received, what has it meant for the risk to the business, what impact has it had on the goals and strategies of the business, what challenges do we still face and what is happening next. Give me the assurance that I am seeking based on what you have done and give me an honest appraisal of what we should be concerned about now and looking ahead.

Make your papers visually impactful. Pages upon pages of words may have been the way it has always been done. But it is time to change that up. As the old saying goes, "a picture paints a thousand words." This is absolutely the case when it comes to Board papers. Use your space wisely. Here are some examples of visuals you should consider:

- **Charts and graphs** – include some colourful bar graphs, pie charts and line graphs to show trending and comparison of data.
- **Heat maps** – use colourful heatmaps to help your reader quickly identify high-risk areas.
- **Tables** – these are easy to read and understand when structured and formatted well.
- **Infographics** – with the help of AI, these can be much easier to create nowadays and will catch the attention of the reader and can really help you to get your message across.
- **Pictures** – yes, I do mean photographs, clippings from articles, newspapers, documents or any other type of pictures. Sometimes, to really get the message across, a digital image of what you want to say can have a real impact. An example of where this could work is with a Health & Safety Internal Audit engagement. If your audit identified some really concerning risks, take pictures whilst performing the audit fieldwork, and include an image or two, or perhaps a collage of images (if there were numerous high-risk findings!). This tactic can really bring risks to life around the boardroom table.
- **Dashboards** – everyone loves a good dashboard nowadays. Why not consider upping your game a level and making it an interactive dashboard? On the assumption (and I am really

hoping this is not the case in your organization) that Board and committee papers are no longer printed and mailed to your Non-Executive Directors, and that they are using their tablets to read and annotate the pack, instead of a static image of your dashboard at a point in time, have it as a live feed, so that readers can click into and interrogate the dashboard to drilldown into the details and interrogate the data that they are most interested in. You can then also use this live version when you are presenting to your Board and Committee.

These ideas will help you in keeping your papers crisp and concise, and make them stand out in the crowd of papers that people will be reading. This allows you to connect with your customer and give the customer what they want (even if sometimes they didn't know they wanted or needed it!)

7.8 Presenting to Your Audit Committee

Your board paper is now looking incredible! That paper is one of your core products. The next element of your product is to actually present your paper to the Board or Audit Committee. This is just as important and therefore requires a significant amount of time and attention. Whilst I am not going to talk about presentation skills here – you will find ample books that cover this much better than I ever could – there are a number of strategies that you should consider adopting to help you make a bold impact:

- **Take the paper as read** – Your paper is well-written, visually impactful and concise. Your readers will have (or should have – it is their job to do so) read it and digested its content. When it comes to presenting, take the papers as read. Please do not begin to start to read out your paper or talk through every paragraph and every detail. Your time is limited, and people's attention spans nowadays are shorter. Instead, use your time wisely. Pull out the salient points in your paper – those key messages that you want to get across – and explain those. Signpost any specifics that you may require, for example, approval of a charter or audit plan, discussion on a certain topic and support for resolving delayed management actions.

Remember, you need to ensure there is time for questions and challenge. That "question and answer" session is a key part of the process when it comes to corporate governance.

- **Rehearse** – Do not just turn up on the morning of the Audit Committee, expecting to simply run through the contents of your paper and get an easy ride. This is your chance to shine in front of some of your most important customers. We have talked a lot earlier in this book about demonstrating competence and building credibility. This is where you do it. But you have to practice. Be prepared for which elements of your paper you will focus on, how you will deliver your messages and how much time you will need. Practice makes perfect. Rehearse when alone – a little easier for many nowadays with the advent of hybrid working. Rehearse in front of a trusted person – and get their honest – and constructive – feedback. Rehearse and record yourself. Watch it back and see what you like and what you dislike. Refine and then do it again. This gives you a chance to consider posture, body language, tone, speed of delivery, etc. It is not an 18-minute TED talk, but you should definitely consider rehearsing as if it were. Over time, you will develop a style and approach you are comfortable with.
- **Know your customer** – Know who you are presenting to. And if you don't know, get to know. Identify who will be in attendance. They may be people that you know well and work closely with. Sometimes, there may be NEDs that you only really see four times a year, that is, during those committee meetings. Find out about their background, experience and interests. The best way is through interacting with them outside of these formal meetings. But you can also look people up on the internet and gain some knowledge from whatever you find that is publicly available. Then tailor your presentation to ensure you are focusing on what your customer is interested in and wants to know. Committee members change over time, so ensure you are keeping on top of this by continuously building up profiles of your customers.
- **Anticipate questions you will be asked** – You know the Q&A is coming directly after – or maybe even during – the

delivery of your presentation. You want to be prepared and be able to answer these questions. There is nothing worse than being asked a question, one that your customer really needs a good answer to, and you stumble when responding. This will quickly shatter their confidence in you. Your NED will be thinking to themselves, surely this CAE knew this question was coming, why can't they give me an answer. As part of your rehearsals, think about what questions you are likely to get asked. Write those questions down. Then write down your answers. The answers need to be concise but also give enough detail to demonstrate that you know what you are talking about. Have a trusted colleague read your paper and identify what questions they would ask. Prepare for all these potential questions. But no matter how hard you prepare, you are still likely to get that curveball question that no one could have predicted. And you still need to answer, and it needs to be a good answer. A good technique here is to have a set of holding statements that you can draw upon. Maybe you need to take the question offline, have more of a think, or research, before coming back with a good answer. This, in my mind, is a perfectly good response. As a NED, I want my question answered, but I may well be happy to wait until later that day or even a day or so, for you to then come back to me – via a quick call or short email – with the answer. Better to get a good, accurate answer than something made up on the spot. Be prepared to take things away, but make sure you respond quickly – and your response answers the question.

- **Know your stuff** – There is nothing more frustrating for a NED than having been taken through a paper by a CAE and then asking a follow-up question for some further detail, and the CAE not having a clue about the detail. Make sure you know your stuff. Even if you haven't written the paper entirely yourself and were not close to all the audit engagements and advisory work contained in the paper, you still need to know the details enough to be able to competently and comprehensively field questions. Get into the details. If you have followed the above steps, that is, rehearsed, understood your customers and anticipated the likely questions, you should be fine. If you are anticipating some detailed questions are likely to come your way on a specific audit engagement, consider having support, that is, the auditor who performed the work, attend for that portion of the meeting. Make sure they are prepped to know their stuff.

7.9 Tailored Solutions = Happy Customers

These end products are what will make or break you with your customers. Constantly innovate and create tailored solutions to delight your customers. That big impact you are seeking will be felt the most based on much of what we have discussed in this chapter and the end products you implement and deliver.

8
Skills, Mindset and Courage

LEARNING OBJECTIVE

The reader will gain an appreciation of the importance of the need for a broad range of skills and how this can be achieved through building in various forms of diversity into their Internal Audit function, the value that can be found in neurodiversity, how to capitalize on the changing workforce and how to develop a mindset of courage!

8.1 The Need for Diverse Skills

In today's world of Internal Audit, it is essential to have a broad range of skills in your arsenal. That means you will need a diverse team to help you succeed. Diversity means lots of different things to different people. It could be socio-economic background, cultural, religious, gender, educational, age, etc.

8.2 The Accountant Turned Internal Auditor

Many will have trodden the familiar path of starting out as trainee accountants, performing external financial audits and then either in their existing firms moving into risk assurance divisions, which involves providing Internal Audit services to clients or moving into industry into an Internal Audit function. This has meant that many Internal Audit teams are predominantly made up of accountants and people with a pure financial background. This was great 20 or even 30 years ago. Back then, most Internal Audit functions were seen as

DOI: 10.1201/9781003519256-8

there to provide assurance over only the finance processes and nothing else. It therefore made complete sense that Internal Auditors needed to have a solid financial background and education.

This is not the case anymore. Internal Audit is not about finance. It is not about checking invoices, reviewing balance sheets and performing audits of payroll or accounts receivables. The assurance that you should be providing is across the entire business, focusing on where the risks to your business are. Yes, at times this will absolutely be a financial risk. But more often than not, it is operational risk, compliance risk or regulatory risk.

In the modern world of Internal Audit, you must be able to provide assurance over your business unit processes, sales and marketing functions, people functions, communications, legal, R&D, manufacturing, business development, health & safety, facilities, estates, information technology, information security, data protection and the list goes on. You simply cannot do this with just accountants.

What is the answer? Diversity of skills, diversity of thinking and diversity of backgrounds and experience. So many large Internal Audit functions and medium-sized Internal Audit functions struggle with getting this right. How on earth can a small Internal Audit shop achieve this?

8.3 Boosting Diversity

There are several innovative ways to boost diversity in your team. Firstly, take some time to find out and understand your existing team. There is likely to be diversity that you were not aware of. There is a need to be considerate and sensitive when discussing this topic. Not everyone will be comfortable to share, and they have no obligation to. But even in a small team, you are likely to find out lots of information that you were not aware of, for example, the different languages your team may speak, countries they have lived in, family background and religious and cultural experiences.

If you are looking to hire, do not fall into the very common trap – and one that I myself have fallen into – which is to hire someone just like you, similar professional background, employment history, interests, etc. Just because you have things in common, have rapport, and they have trodden the same path as you, does not make them an ideal fit. It does not bring anything new to the table. I am not talking about ethnicity, gender, age or religion here. All these could be different from you, but you still end up hiring your doppelganger. Do not fall into this trap.

When hiring, you don't just need a job description; you need a skills gap analysis to really help you identify what you and your organization need, before you begin looking. Far too often, I see that the first mandatory requirement for an Internal Audit position is "relevant qualification," which then goes on to list finance or accountancy qualifications. If you are a one-person Internal Audit function and you are lucky enough to get the budget to recruit one or more additional headcount, why would you look for another accountant who has the same skills as you? Your next few audits are on R&D, manufacturing, information security, supply chain, business development – and you are going to hire an accountant to perform these audits? Just doesn't make sense.

We talked about guest auditors and secondments in Chapter 4. This is another brilliant way to boost diversity in your Internal Audit function. When you look at your upcoming Internal Audit engagements and advisory work, look across your organization. And you may well find the diverse set of skills you need is readily available. You can teach them the auditing part, and it is their other skills that you need them to bring to the table. And that is what will really move the needle when it comes to delivering value in the output of that audit engagement.

In my time, where I have been lucky enough to have guest auditors join me and my teams for audit engagements, they have made invaluable contributions. Even if they have never audited before. Here are a couple of examples.

I had an audit of a third-party partner that our business worked with in a particular country where we did not want to expand into by setting up a subsidiary. We had a plan to audit a number of these partners each year, taking a risk-based approach as to which ones we visit. I had never been to this country before and was unfamiliar with the culture and language. None of my team had the relevant language and cultural experience either. However, we knew that there was someone from the Legal team who was a dual national of this country. They had no experience in Internal Audit, and no interest in Internal

Audit. However, they thought they definitely had some transferable skills that would be extremely beneficial to make the audit a success. This particular audit engagement was even more sensitive, as we were auditing a third-party business. This guest auditor jumped at the chance of helping us, as it meant a chance for them to visit home and family whilst on this business trip. Whilst on audit, our guest auditor proved to be worth their weight in gold. They not only understood the language, which helped with meetings and interviews, but also with reviewing documents. What was even more valuable was their understanding of the culture and, therefore, their ability to question when something did not feel right and their ability to challenge, but in a manner that was appropriate and resonated with the people we were auditing. Outside of the day-to-day auditing at the offices, they were able to help in terms of navigating travel, logistics, etc. It made what could have been a dangerous and daunting audit into a safe and fun experience. Both the internal auditors and the guest auditor gained a great deal from the experience.

Another example was again an audit of a third-party partner in a country where we had limited exposure. However, this time, our guest auditor was someone from the Quality Assurance function. This was a second-line function that performed a very specific technical audit of product quality, and the processes our third parties used to manufacture, store and distribute our product. Similar to Internal Audit, the Quality Assurance function had a risk-based audit plan to audit a number of these third parties each year. The timing of our Internal Audit and the Quality Assurance audit was very close, and after some discussion between our two functions and the third-party partner, we all agreed that we would perform a joint audit. This was a great result for the third-party, as rather than having two sets of auditors come out at different times, they would just have one visit and conduct both audits simultaneously. It was also great for our Internal Audit team as they were able to learn the methodology and execution of a Quality Assurance audit, and vice versa. Both teams were able to learn new skills and knowledge. And both teams came away from this experience with a stronger working relationship to build on going forward. It showed senior management that the second-line and third-line were actively talking to each other and proactively working together to provide assurance, but in a more efficient manner. For me, this is a wonderful example of how joint audits with other assurance functions can deliver diversity.

As a small team or a one-person team, if you have a great co-source partner to support your function, this is another source of diversity. Co-source naturally brings diversity by virtue of the model itself. You may have a core co-source team, that is, an audit partner and an account director. But each time you perform an audit engagement, given the wide array of topics, you will find yourself with different audit teams each time. These audit teams will comprise different socio-economic backgrounds, cultures, religions, genders and ages. This diversity will be seen by your clients and the business as a whole. Matching the right auditors to the audit engagement topics brings diversity of ideas that would never be possible in a small in-house team alone. The diversity from co-source brings a real strength to your in-house function.

8.4 Personality Traits

Personality traits are another consideration when we think about diversity. Auditors tend to be analytical, questioning, cautious and formal. Yes, this is a serious generalization! I know we do not all have these personality traits. But more often than not, if you were to perform a personality trait test on you and your team, I bet that this personality trait will be the dominant one.

This is another example of where we, as Internal Audit, need diversity. We need a mix of personality traits to succeed. So, we definitely need the analytical types, but we also need the following types of people:

- Assertive, competitive and decisive
- Enthusiastic, persuasive and energetic
- Patient, encouraging and caring

Why does the mix matter? It gives you a better balance of skills and perspectives.

- You can ask the tough questions and push for action, but also build rapport with stakeholders, influence senior leaders, whilst approaching sensitive situations carefully.

- Your stakeholders vary, and so you can deploy the right team member(s) to ensure you connect effectively.
- Different traits can bring different energy and stop you from playing it too safe – and help you spot opportunities that you yourself may not have ever seen.

There is no right mix, or optimal mix, but working on having a mix of personality traits will result in increased influence and ability to drive change. And that is what Internal Audit is there to do in a business.

Hopefully, this has opened your eyes to new and innovative ways to improve and build diversity into your team, and into the work you do. And by doing this, you will see it pay huge dividends in terms of the value you bring to your business. And importantly, how you and your function are seen by the wider business and the C-suite. They will be so impressed, they will be asking other teams in your business why they aren't following your lead and learning from you.

This is another example of real, tangible, highly visible value that your Internal Audit function will bring.

8.5 Equity and Inclusion

We've talked about the D – diversity. Let's talk about the E and the I – Equity and Inclusion. Equity refers to the fair treatment, access and opportunity for all individuals, ensuring that systemic barriers are identified and addressed. It emphasizes the need to provide tailored resources and support to achieve equal outcomes for marginalized groups. Inclusion refers to the practice of creating environments in which all individuals feel valued, respected and empowered to contribute fully, regardless of their diverse backgrounds or identities. It involves actively fostering a culture that embraces differences and encourages participation from everyone.

Let's consider what that means for an Internal Audit function.

When it comes to Equity, you may wish to explicitly call out the promotion of fairness and impartiality in your policies and procedures. Understand how bias could creep into your audit methodology and audit work, and identify where this may be the case, and how it can be addressed. You may wish to consider adopting an inclusive decision-making process for some activities to allow a more comprehensive understanding and enhance trust in your teams. To support inclusion, actively seek out a variety of perspectives from a variety of people. Encourage open communication and take the time to listen and act upon what you learn. This allows your team to feel empowered to contribute and develop.

You can be a leader in your organization in driving this forward by adopting these and your own ideas with a focus on demonstrating and showcasing the tangible benefits they bring to your organization as a whole.

8.6 Neurodiversity

8.6.1 Understanding Neurodiversity

Neurodiversity is a concept that recognizes and respects the natural variations in human brain function and behaviour. The term encompasses a range of neurological differences, including autism, ADHD, dyslexia, dyspraxia and other cognitive variations. These differences are not deficits or disorders; they are opportunities to identify unique perspectives that individuals with these abilities bring to the table.

8.6.2 Neurodiversity in the Workplace

In your workplace, think about how you can embrace neurodiversity by creating an inclusive environment where individuals with differences can thrive. This involves recognizing the diverse ways in which people think, process information and solve problems. Be accepting and supportive and lead your team in setting an example for them to follow. Make the effort to tap into the full potential of these employees.

8.6.3 The Positives of Neurodiversity in Corporate Internal Audit

Neurodiversity can bring numerous benefits to a corporate Internal Audit function. Here are a few positives that I have experienced in my time:

Enhanced Problem-Solving and Innovation: Neurodiverse individuals can possess unique problem-solving abilities and innovative thinking. Their different perspectives can surface creative solutions and new approaches to complex issues that you would have never identified by yourself. Attention to detail and pattern recognition skills are examples that can prove invaluable in identifying anomalies and potential risks during audits. This can be particularly beneficial in tasks that require precision and accuracy, such as reviewing financial statements, interrogating data sets and identifying discrepancies.

Improved Analytical Skills: Many neurodiverse individuals excel in analytical thinking and data analysis. Intense focus on specific tasks and strong spatial reasoning skills can enable people to see connections and relationships that others might overlook.

Diverse Perspectives: A neurodiverse team brings a variety of viewpoints and approaches to risk and audit. This diversity can enhance the overall quality of the audit process by challenging assumptions and encouraging critical thinking. I have seen it help in identifying blind spots and uncovering risks that would otherwise have gone unnoticed by me.

Increased Resilience and Adaptability: Neurodiverse individuals often develop strong coping mechanisms and resilience due to the challenges they face. This adaptability should be seen as an asset in a dynamic Internal Audit function.

8.6.4 Creating an Inclusive Environment

You will need to think differently too, if you want to get the best from your neurodiverse team. It is essential to create an inclusive workplace environment. This involves implementing supportive policies and practices, such as:

- Flexible Work Arrangements: Offering flexible work hours and remote work options can accommodate the needs of neurodiverse employees, allowing them to work in environments where they feel most comfortable and productive.
- Clear Communication: Providing clear and concise instructions, as well as regular feedback, can help neurodiverse individuals understand expectations and perform at their best.

People communicate in different ways and have different preferences. Understand what works best and adapt accordingly.
- Awareness: Raise awareness about neurodiversity and educate employees on how to support their neurodiverse colleagues.
- Accommodations and Adjustments: Making reasonable accommodations, such as providing noise-cancelling headphones, creating quiet workspaces and allowing the use of assistive technology, can help neurodiverse employees thrive.

None of this is a big deal. All of it is pretty straightforward and simple to do. Do not make a big deal out of really immaterial changes. People evolve, and so should your Internal Audit function. Give people the opportunity for them to give you their best.

8.6.5 The Value of Neurodiversity

Embracing neurodiversity in the Internal Audit function enhances the quality and effectiveness of Internal Audits and contributes to a more inclusive and innovative workplace culture. It helps organizations build stronger, more resilient teams that are better equipped to navigate the complexities of today's business world.

It demonstrates a commitment to social responsibility and ethical practices. This can enhance the company's reputation and attract top talent. But it is just the right thing to do.

Neurodiversity is a valuable asset that can transform the Internal Audit function and contribute to the success of an entire organization. Embracing neurodiversity can unlock new opportunities for growth and innovation.

8.7 Emotional Intelligence

8.7.1 Understanding Emotional Intelligence (EQ)

EQ refers to the ability to recognize, understand, manage and influence one's own emotions and the emotions of others. These are skills such as self-awareness, self-regulation, motivation, empathy and social skills. For as long as I can remember, our focus has been on cognitive intelligence (IQ), which measures intellectual abilities. EQ focuses on emotional and social competencies that are crucial for effective interpersonal interactions and leadership. Better interactions and leading the way are core to a successful Internal Audit activity, so it seems strange to me that EQ has not been a focus.

8.7.2 EQ in Business Today

In today's fast-paced, global business environment, EQ has become increasingly important. Let's take some time to understand the key reasons why EQ is essential in today's workplace:

1. **Better Communication**: High EQ individuals are adept at understanding and managing their own emotions, which allows them to communicate more effectively. They have learned how to convey their thoughts and ideas clearly, listen actively and respond empathetically to their customers and colleagues. Better communication leads to better collaboration, reduced misunderstandings and stronger relationships.
2. **Leadership**: Leaders with high EQ are equipped to inspire and motivate their teams. They can build trust, foster a positive work environment and understand how to navigate complex interpersonal dynamics. These high EQ leaders drive higher levels of engagement and performance.
3. **Conflict Resolution**: Conflict is inevitable in any workplace and is part and parcel of being an internal auditor. Individuals with high EQ can manage and resolve conflicts more effectively. They can remain calm under pressure, empathize with different perspectives, and find mutually beneficial solutions. Sounds like exactly what I want from an internal auditor.
4. **Adaptability and Resilience**: High EQ individuals are more adaptable and resilient in the face of change and adversity. They can demonstrate the ability to manage stress, stay focused and maintain a positive outlook even in challenging situations.
5. **Better Decision-Making**: High EQ people can balance logic and emotions, consider the impact of their decisions on others, and make more informed and empathetic choices. This means better outcomes and more ethical decision-making.

8.7.3 The Role of EQ in Internal Audit

EQ is particularly valuable for internal auditors and here are some ways in which high EQ can benefit:

1. Building trust and rapport
2. Effective communication of findings
3. Managing resistance and conflict
4. Enhancing team dynamics
5. Adapting to organizational culture

8.7.4 Creating an EQ-Friendly Environment

To fully harness the benefits of EQ in Internal Audit, you must work to create an environment that supports and nurtures EQ. Here are some practical ways to do this:

- **Training and Development**: Provide training and development opportunities focused on building EQ skills. This can include workshops, coaching and mentoring programs that help auditors enhance their self-awareness, empathy and communication skills.
- **Encouraging Self-Reflection**: Encourage auditors to engage in self-reflection and self-assessment. This can help them identify their strengths and areas for improvement in terms of EQ. Regular feedback and performance reviews will also support this process.
- **Promoting and Rewarding High EQ**: Foster a positive work culture that values and rewards EQ. Recognize and celebrate behaviours that demonstrate high EQ, such as effective communication, empathy and conflict resolution.
- **Providing Supportive Resources**: Offer resources and support systems that help internal auditors manage stress and maintain their emotional well-being.

8.7.5 The Value of High EQ in Internal Audit

EQ is a valuable asset that can significantly enhance the effectiveness of an Internal Audit function. High EQ auditors can build trust, communicate effectively, manage conflicts and adapt to different organizational cultures. These are all assets that you will want and need. Foster an environment that supports and nurtures EQ. Use it to unlock the full potential of your Internal Audit teams and drive better outcomes for you and your business as a whole.

8.8 The Changing Workforce

There is a need for business leaders to understand, plan for and adapt their requirements and expectations to the ever-changing workforce. Given the pace of change in the business world, advice on this topic continues to change at an ever-increasing pace. So, the only real advice here is to focus on keeping pace with that change. Without an understanding of the pool of potential candidates and what their expectations, beliefs and needs are, you will find it harder and harder to recruit.

Marcus Panton, Global Director & Co-founder of the Audit Risk & Recruitment Company (ARRC), sums up the challenge:

> The workforce of today is far more interested in the value proposition you and your organization brings. They want to know that they are doing something which has purpose. And in truth, this can be good for society. The trend has really shifted in a direction that many hiring managers may find hard to be able to understand or relate to.
>
> The new generation has completely moved away from blind loyalty and commitment to a company. They are far less afraid to work for a company for two or three years and then move on. There is an expectation of flexibility, and that is not simply about working from home more. It is a move to a model of portfolio careers, where they are not beholden to one organization, but want to sell themselves out to multiple organizations. It is an inevitability of the gig economy work model that we are all now becoming accustomed to; but that is now expanding into professions that many thought it would not expand to.
>
> With platforms such as LinkedIn, workers now have access to information on every company and every potential role currently available in the market, in their region, in their country, and across the entire world. They are flooded with choice.

Hiring managers need to understand and adapt to this to attract and retain the best people.

8.9 Mindset – Courage

Skills, experience, knowledge and diversity are not enough. The final piece of the puzzle is mindset, and with that, for us internal auditors, must come courage. Courage to learn, courage to think outside of the box, courage to get things wrong and courage to challenge. And ultimately, if the situation calls for it, the courage to walk away.

Based on his many years of experience in hiring Heads of Internal Audit into medium and large companies, Marcus captures this sentiment perfectly with the following valuable perspective:

> The candidates that have impressed me the most are the ones that are bold and are not afraid to push boundaries and challenge, and not simply accept the status quo. These are the candidates that push back and challenge. This may even be during the interview process. They do not just accept what they're being told or accept what they're being given. The idea isn't to just fit in. The idea is a business is hiring you because you can make change happen.
>
> Two of the most important skills you need are commercial acumen and Emotional Intelligence.
>
> And then just keep ruffling feathers. As soon as you get too comfortable, you start to lose impact.

9
Small Teams, BIG Impact!

9.1 Turning Ideas into Reality

We have covered a lot of ground in this book, and as we reach the end of this journey through the innovative world of Internal Audit, take some time to reflect on the ideas we have explored and the actionable strategies that we need to take forward. I wanted to write this book so that it could be used as a practical guide to reimagining Internal Audit, especially for small teams, and it is now up to you to take these ideas and turn them into reality.

9.2 The Power of Small Teams

Throughout these eight chapters, our focus has been on the immense impact that small Internal Audit teams can have. Size does not have to limit your ability to make a significant difference in your organization. By leveraging creativity, strategic thinking and innovative approaches, you and your team can deliver high-quality assurance and advisory services that rival those of larger functions. All that we have learned is not reserved for those smaller teams but should be harnessed by teams of all shapes and sizes. It is about quality over quantity. The value you bring through insight and foresight is what truly matters.

9.3 Building Strong Foundations

We have discussed the importance of establishing a solid foundation for your Internal Audit function. This includes defining clear terms of reference, structuring your team effectively, following the GIAS and its thorough guidance and ensuring robust governance arrangements. Set these foundations, and you will create a framework that supports your team's success and enables you to navigate whatever challenges come your way with confidence.

DOI: 10.1201/9781003519256-9

9.4 Leveraging Technology and Third-Party Support

Innovation is at the heart of modern Internal Audit, and technology plays a critical role in this transformation. From data analytics to AI-powered tools, embracing technology will enhance your efficiency, improve the quality of your outputs and provide deeper insights into your organization's risks and opportunities. Do not be afraid to take those risks and seize those opportunities.

Utilizing third-party support through co-sourcing can bring fresh perspectives and specialized expertize to your team. Your co-source partner is just that – a partner, an extension to your team. Learn to get the most value out of them.

9.5 Systemizing for Consistency and Efficiency

Consistency is key to providing your customers with high-quality Internal Audit services. By systemizing your processes, creating standardized templates and automating routine tasks, you can ensure that your team operates efficiently and consistently. This not only improves the quality of your work but also frees up time for those value-added activities and outputs that will delight your customers.

9.6 Expanding Your Role and Impact

Internal Audit is not confined to traditional assurance activities. We have explored how you can take on additional roles, such as Risk Management and Counter-Fraud services, to broaden your impact and provide wider value to your organization. Being brave and embracing these roles will demonstrate your versatility and commitment to keeping your organization safe.

9.7 Engaging and Impressing Stakeholders

Effective communication and stakeholder engagement are essential for Internal Audit success. It is an area that is often overlooked, and has resulted in a lack of visibility, understanding and credibility. Branding and marketing your function, delivering innovative outputs and becoming a trusted advisor to the C-suite and Audit Committee are all strategies that can elevate your function's profile and influence. You must carve out time to work on impressing your stakeholders – through your audit engagements, advisory services and business foresight. Build strong and meaningful relationships that allow your function to flourish.

9.8 Embracing Diversity and Inclusion

A diverse and inclusive Internal Audit team will bring a wealth of perspectives, experiences and skills that can drive innovation and enhance your function's effectiveness. Work hard to foster a culture of diversity, equity and inclusion, and you will create an environment where everyone feels valued and empowered to contribute their best. Be a leader in this, demonstrate the tangible value it brings, and inspire your organization to always move forward.

9.9 The Courage to Lead

Finally, leading an innovative Internal Audit function requires courage. Courage to challenge the status quo, to push boundaries and to continuously improve. You must adopt a mindset that embraces change, takes risks and inspires your team to do the same. It may not have been on the job description when you applied for the role, but being courageous is now an integral part of our job description.

9.10 Step Forward with Confidence

Armed with the insights and strategies from this book, you have the tools to transform your Internal Audit function and make a lasting impact on your organization. Actually, not just your organization, but also an impact on you, your team and the wider profession.

Do not try everything at once. Start by implementing the ideas that resonate most with you. Then, gradually implement more ideas, and these can and should be ideas of your own. But, whatever you decide upon, do not overthink it – just START.

Remember, the journey of Internal Audit excellence is ongoing. Keep seeking out opportunities for improvement, follow those emerging trends and never stop learning. Do this, and you will not only elevate your Internal Audit function but also tangibly contribute to the overall success of your organization.

Step forward with confidence. Embrace the future of Internal Audit. Make a BIG impact!

Index

For Product Safety Concerns and Information please contact our EU
representative GPSR@taylorandfrancis.com
Taylor & Francis Verlag GmbH, Kaufingerstraße 24, 80331 München, Germany

www.ingramcontent.com/pod-product-compliance
Ingram Content Group UK Ltd.
Pitfield, Milton Keynes, MK11 3LW, UK
UKHW020208200926
475702UK00004B/664

* 9 7 8 1 0 3 2 8 4 2 3 5 6 *